D0777363

TO _____

FROM _____

I HAVE LOVED YOU
WITH AN EVERLASTING LOVE.

JEREMIAH 31:3

Fiercely

LOVED

GOD'S WILD

THOUGHTS

ABOUT YOU

LISA BEVERE

Revell
a division of Baker Publishing Group
Grand Rapids, Michigan

© 2022 by Lisa Bevere

Published by Revell
a division of Baker Publishing Group
PO Box 6287, Grand Rapids, MI 49516-6287
www.revellbooks.com

Printed in the United States of America

Library of Congress Cataloging-in-Publication Data
Names: Bevere, Lisa, author.
Title: Fiercely loved : God's wild thoughts about you / Lisa Bevere.
Description: Grand Rapids : Revell, a division of Baker Publishing Group, [2022]
Identifiers: LCCN 2021052145 | ISBN 9780800741709 (cloth) | ISBN 9781493437450 (ebook)
Subjects: LCSH: God (Christianity)—Love—Meditations. | Christian women—Religious
    life—Meditations.
Classification: LCC BT140 .B485 2022 | DDC 231/.6—dc23/eng/20211118
LC record available at https://lccn.loc.gov/2021052145

Some of the material in this devotional is taken from *Without Rival* (2016) and *Adamant* (2018) by Lisa Bevere.

The author is represented by The FEDD Agency, Inc.

Baker Publishing Group publications use paper produced from sustainable forestry practices and post-consumer waste whenever possible.

22 23 24 25 26 27 28   7 6 5 4 3 2

CONTENTS

ONE

FIERCELY LOVED

For love is strong as death.

Song of Solomon 8:6

Fiercely Loved. Did the title quicken a spark of hope within you? Or did you immediately disqualify yourself from such an intense promise?

Either way, a deep knowing that you are fiercely loved is vital. Because it changes everything.

You see, there is nothing passive or indifferent when it comes to how your Creator feels about you. We've all heard the phrase "Jesus loves you" so many times that it has become white noise. But when was the last time you felt his love wash over you and lift you when you thought you least deserved it? His love is not just words; it is life. A love that is larger, wilder, and more dangerous than anything we've ever known or experienced. A love far vaster than the sum of all expressions of human love. God doesn't *have* love for you. He *is* love for you. He is not merely *in* love with you. You are immersed in his love. And once it touches you . . . you are never the same.

His love consumes and refines even as it comforts and restores.

I understand that by attaching *fiercely* to *loved*, I added a measure of danger, making it sound as though this love would threaten to consume the objects of its affection. Understandably, this pairing of *fierce* and *love* is a wild and rare one. At a bare minimum, this type of love would leave its mark on us. We glimpse this coupling in this poetic verse:

> Set me as a seal upon your heart,
>> as a seal upon your arm,
> for love is strong as death,
>> jealousy is fierce as the grave.
> Its flashes are flashes of fire,
>> the very flame of the LORD. (Song of Sol. 8:6)

Love *as strong as death* and jealousy *as fierce as the grave* are beyond any human's capacity to maintain. A love of this type of intensity can be ascribed only to the One who first made us, then gave his all to prove his love for us. But don't imagine that my use of the word *us* means that this love is fractured and fragmented into lesser individual pieces. His love is all-consuming and indivisible.

I am fiercely loved.

11

TWO

ALWAYS IN GOD'S THOUGHTS

How precious to me are your thoughts, O God!
How vast is the sum of them!
If I would count them, they are more than the sand.
I awake, and I am still with you.

Psalm 139:17–18

Now, let's talk about those thoughts. "Your thoughts" here refers to our Father's thoughts. It's true that God Most High has ideas about you that are so rare and beautiful they are outside our human comprehension. What is he thinking? Thoughts of love. Thoughts of joy. Thoughts of peace. Thoughts of grace. Thoughts of mercy. Thoughts of creation. Thoughts of goodness. Thoughts of care.

Not only are these thoughts precious; they are innumerable. The task of beginning to number God's thoughts is just as impossible as counting the sands of the seas. His thoughts never leave us; they are as constant as his love. Fiercely loved one, you have always been, you are, and you will always be on his mind.

And yet we rarely imagine that we are seen this way. These thoughts are the very antithesis of how we've learned to see ourselves. I was raised to believe that God was distant and disappointed. But in David's words, we hear something unexpected; we hear wonder. David reveled in the wild truth that God actually treasured him. Alone in the wilderness, David had come to know the Most High as an intimate friend and confidant, someone who loved him and loved being with him.

> When I look at your heavens, the work of your fingers,
> > the moon and the stars, which you have set in place,
> what is man that you are mindful of him,
> > and the son of man that you care for him? (Ps. 8:3–4)

Beholding the wonder, David pondered why God would notice him. God's thoughts are always about his largeness rather than our smallness. Our Father has never been disappointed by the thought of you. You are his idea. He created you. He loves you. He gave his Son to redeem you because you are always on his mind.

I believe my Father's thoughts toward me are wildly wonderful.

THREE

WILD ABOUT YOU

Be here—the king is wild for you. Since he's your lord, adore him.

Psalm 45:11 Message

I pray this verse challenges the way you think God thinks about you. Lovely one, don't be afraid; only believe this sentiment is for you and be present. The God who is truth cannot lie. He is wild about you . . . and that doesn't make him crazy. But you'd be crazy not to accept his gift of fierce love. As a daughter of your Lord, you are under his rule. His rule is love. One way you can honor his lordship is by choosing to accept how he feels about you. His love for you is not subject to how you feel about yourself. His love is selfless. He is love. His love is independent of how we look, feel, or act. We might as well surrender to this love that is beyond our comprehension.

Did you wonder why I chose the word *wild* to describe God's thoughts about you? Let's examine some of the adjectives that describe the term *wild*: exciting, thrilling, enthusiastic, wind-swept, untamed, uncontrollable, fierce, outrageous, unmanageable, unconventional, and reckless.

Let's pause and ponder the application of these descriptors.

The revelation that the God who is love loves you is exciting. If you are bored with the idea that God loves you, it's because you've heard it but never experienced it.

This realization that he constantly thinks of you is thrilling and should awaken a fresh enthusiasm in every aspect of your walk with the Father. The combined imagery of being untamed, uncontrollable, fierce, outrageous, unmanageable, unconventional, and reckless flies in the face of every sedated man-made religion. It reminds me of a quote about Aslan from *The Lion, the Witch and the Wardrobe*: "He's wild, you know. Not like a tame lion."[*]

The God Most High, Creator of the heavens and earth, is not a manageable deity that we control or manipulate. Nor is God a man that he should lie (see Num. 23:19). He means what he has said about you. His heart is set on you, and nothing you do or say can remove his seal of love from you. In Christ, his love is forever settled. It is now time for you to settle it for yourself.

> *God is wild for me,*
> *and I adore him for it.*

[*] C. S. Lewis, *The Lion, the Witch and the Wardrobe* (Grand Rapids: Zondervan, 2009), 168.

FOUR

THE GOD WHO HOVERS

In the beginning, God created the heavens and the earth. The earth was without form and void, and darkness was over the face of the deep. And the Spirit of God was hovering over the face of the waters.

Genesis 1:1–2

Our God is the Creator. When the earth was held captive and its wonder buried by fathoms of darkness that made it a formless void, God drew near. The Spirit of God hovered over the face of the shadowed globe.

Let's pause with this idea of hovering. *Rachaf* is the Hebrew word meaning to hover, and it is best translated as "to linger or to float in a manner that is at once gentle and cherishing." I can't help but envision the tenderness of a mother as she pauses over the bed of her beloved child tossing fretfully in the throes of a nightmare. The mother whispers words of comfort to pull her child from darkness's grasp: "I am here. Wake up; it is only a bad dream."

Perhaps you find yourself in the grip of shadowed fears that have made your life feel void of purpose. What once was clear now looms before you unclear and formless. I have good news for you. Our Creator didn't just hover; he spoke.

And God said, "Let there be light," and there was light. (Gen. 1:3)

I believe God is speaking light into any and every formless, void space in your life. Your Creator speaks to what could be, what should be in your life.

The Spirit of God still hovers. He is as close as your breath and longs to gather you close and whisper light and love. You belong to him. He is the one who heals your brokenness and fulfills your deepest need for intimacy. Whatever chaos is swirling in you, God is hovering and ready to speak life and light over you. Fiercely loved one, invite the Spirit of God to speak light into every shadowed, formless space.

> *The Spirit of God is near,*
> *speaking life and light over me.*

FIVE

WHO YOU ARE

Fear not, for I have redeemed you;
I have called you by name, you are mine.

Isaiah 43:1

God calls each of us by name, not by a group label. Knowing *who you are* is vastly more important than knowing where you are going or even what you can do. Because he is your Creator, God has quite a bit to say to you about who you are. And who you truly are carries within it the revelation of what you could be.

We cannot afford to doubt our God-assigned, unique destiny. If we do, we will undermine with hesitancy, fear, or anger all that has been entrusted to us. God wants to redeem, restore, and change your identity so that there is no incident, season, or name from your past left to define you. Yes, seasons, criticisms, and events can refine you—they have the potential to shape the mettle of your life—but they are not the substance of your life . . . God is.

You were sincerely sought because you are uniquely loved and you are a unique expression of God's love to others. All that your identity as a child of

God means is just beginning to be expressed as you become who he created you to be. In times of great confusion, Hebrews 12:2 tells us to "[look] unto Jesus the author and finisher of our faith" (KJV).

In a world in which everyone is trying to discover or remake themselves, he is finishing what he authored. This is your invitation to pursue him . . . that he might reveal you!

It's wild that I am named rather than labeled.

What you have and what you do and who surrounds you can change, but it is vitally important that you never lose who you are or the Creator to whom you belong.

SIX

CHOSEN

> For he knew all about us before we were born and he destined us
> from the beginning to share the likeness of his Son.
>
> Romans 8:29 TPT

You were known and loved before you ever came to be. God was proud of you before you ever knew he existed.

You were not chosen the day you turned to Christ—that is the day you chose. No, my friend, you were chosen in Christ long before the fountains of the deep were formed. You were formed in Christ so that, through the power of transformation, he might be formed in you. You came alive to this truth the day you were born again. Through the death of God's Son, love not only rescued you but also restored you to his initial hope.

Not only are you fiercely loved now, but the foreordained day is coming when you will see him and realize his love has made you look like him! It is his love that transforms you from who you were to who you were always meant to be. No one can keep this kind of love quiet!

You can be secure in this love because God wrapped you in the unstained innocence of Christ long before Adam and Eve had the chance to strip themselves of light and truth and robe themselves in the serpent's shrouds of sin and death. Revelation 13:8 tells us that Jesus was the Lamb slain before the earth was founded. You are not an add-on, an afterthought, or someone who was included at the last minute. You have *always* been welcome.

> It is wild that before I chose God,
> I'd been chosen.

We did not happen to be—we were chosen by God to exist.

—Mother Angelica

SEVEN

BELONGING

> Look with wonder at the depth of the Father's marvelous love that
> he has lavished on us! He has called us and made us his very own
> *beloved* children.
>
> 1 John 3:1 TPT

To know who you are, I don't need to know who you hang around with. I don't need the name of your parents, school, or employer. I want to know the name of the One who gave his life to purchase you. And yet you are missing out on so much if you imagine the reach of his sacrifice stops there. When he found you, he didn't brush you off and put you back where you were before. He raised you and graced you with his righteousness.

Say it now, even if it is but a whisper of your heart: *I am his and he is mine.*

Your eternal Father is the only one who has the right to define you. Your mother conceived, carried, and cared for you, but your heavenly Father conceptualized, created, and spoke you into existence. When you were lost, he redeemed you so he could once again call you his own. The day will come when time as we know it will end; then he will regenerate each of us, and we will realize this earth life was but a seed, and there in heaven we will blossom into our truest form.

I don't know where life has you right now, but please understand that locations, seasons, and circumstances are constantly changing. What really matters in the midst of all the ebb and flow is who you are and to whom you belong.

I cannot help but marvel at his wild, fierce love for me.

Your heavenly Father conceptualized, created, and spoke you into existence.

EIGHT

DAUGHTER

> I will be a father to you,
>> and you shall be sons and daughters to me,
> says the Lord Almighty.
>
> 2 Corinthians 6:18

One thing God cannot do is lie. He will not repeat the lies others have spoken over you. He will not allow a label to be your limit. With him, every label falls away, even the ones you've written on yourself.

He calls you by name, not the names you've been called.

He's been face-to-face with your deepest longings and darkest fears.

He sees the unformed places.

He sees the disappointed hope.

He hears the cries of the frightened and the lonely.

He feels the pain of the shunned and the isolated.

He sees the heaving tumult of humanity in crisis.

He sees the snare of sin and shame.

He sees through the fathoms of darkness that grayed the color of your world.

God sees all of this and speaks light.

Others may call you "girl." He calls you "daughter."

Others may call you a failure. He calls you "daughter."

You may call yourself heterosexual, transgender, asexual, lesbian, or any other of a vast assortment of labels. He calls you his own.

An identity as daughter of the Most High God is higher and reaches deeper than gender, deeper than your worst failures, and deeper than even your wildest dreams.

It is wild how he knows all,
yet calls me daughter.

NINE

YOU ARE A DELIGHT TO GOD

You formed my innermost being, shaping my delicate inside
and my intricate outside,
and wove them all together in my mother's womb.
I thank you, God, for making me so mysteriously complex!
Everything you do is marvelously breathtaking.

Psalm 139:13–14 TPT

You are uniquely loved because you were uniquely created.

Unique means "the sole example of, prototype or only one," and, my favorite definition, "*without equal or rival*." Our Father God stands alone, without rival, so we shouldn't be surprised that in his eyes, we are daughters without rival. This eliminates every reason that we should ever compete with one another.

You are the only example of you!

You are the beginning and the end of you. There is no rival for the way you express God's love to others or for the way he expresses his love to you. No one can do *you* like *you*!

God uniquely created your DNA and knit your frame in secret so he could surprise the world. He authored how your heart expresses itself; he was the architect of your smile and the melody of your voice; he made all your features with the fondest thoughts of only you in mind. He celebrated along with your parents your first smile and watched with affection your first steps.

Because of this tender, intentional care, there are multiple facets of your life that express love uniquely. He wove all these exceptional aspects and specific talents into the package of you, his daughter. He knew each attribute would be expressed best through your feminine form.

God knew you would represent and relate to him best as a daughter. This is the very reason he chose female for your gender. There is a very tender bond between fathers and daughters.

He didn't have another daughter in mind when he fashioned you . . . you are his delight.

I was wildly woven in wonder.

TEN

YOU ARE MORE

From now on, therefore, we regard no one according to the flesh.

2 Corinthians 5:16

*O*ur God is intimate. He knows our fears and speaks directly into our spirits. He has forgotten our sin and shame and buried our transgressions in a sea of forgetfulness. But he remembers those moments that made him smile, the very ones we have forgotten.

We lose sight of our identities when we attach them to the wrong imagery. We lose our abilities when we allow fear and even the pain of others to bury our gifts. When you can run and hide in him, he will speak truth to the most intimate places of your heart:

You are so much more than what you or others can see or touch.

You are so much more than what you've known or done.

You are so much more than what others think about you or even what you think about yourself.

You could never be accurately measured by what you own or lack.

You are more than the span of your years, and you cannot be tethered to the adages of young or old.

You are more than single, divorced, widowed, or married.

You are far more than your gender.

You are a child of the eternal realm.

Those attributes are tangible expressions of the structure that houses the real life that is you. They represent how your life appears to be, but they are not your source of life.

I am wildly more than can be described here and now.

ELEVEN

WATERFALL OF GRACE

> For it was *always* in his perfect plan to adopt us as his delightful
> children . . . so that his tremendous love that cascades over us would
> glorify his grace—for the same love he has for the Beloved, Jesus,
> he has for us.
>
> Ephesians 1:5–6 TPT, emphasis added

Your adoption into God's family was planned from the very beginning. He didn't bring you near because he felt sorry for you or because no one else wanted you. He delights in you because in Christ he sees what you will be rather than what you have been.

I love the word imagery in the verse above . . . *cascades*. I can't help but picture a waterfall. Have you ever stood under one? The water tumbles over you with unrestrained force and in immeasurable amounts. The outflow of God's tremendous grace anoints those who draw near through his love. And a waterfall is no trickle:

Since we are now joined to Christ, we have been given the treasures of redemption by his blood—the total cancellation of our sins—all because of the *cascading riches of his grace*. (Eph. 1:7 TPT, emphasis added)

Outside of Christ, I wouldn't deserve a drop of grace or mercy. I would deserve only the full weight and stain of far more sins than I could even remember to confess. That is who I am outside of him. And yet . . .

His love for us is as intimate as the breath we draw and as far-reaching as the wind that wraps the globe.

His love for us is exclusive and unique.

His love for us is all-inclusive. There is no part of us that escapes his love. He loves us without exception.

I am overwhelmed by this wild waterfall of grace.

TWELVE

WILLING HEARTS

> O Jerusalem, Jerusalem, the city that kills the prophets and stones those who are sent to it! How often would I have gathered your children together as a hen gathers her brood under her wings, and you were not willing!
>
> Matthew 23:37

The Spirit of God is as close to us as a whisper, waiting to gather us to his heart. This longing of the Creator's heart was echoed in the above words of Jesus.

How tragic are the words "you were not willing"?

Even now, the Spirit of God hovers, waiting to speak peace to the storms and to silence the cries of your howling wastelands. He waits, longing to encircle you with the protection and warmth of his wings. Are you willing? Will you invite the Holy Spirit who hovers to draw near? Will you allow him to cover you? Will you persist with your attempts to cover yourself even as you uncover others? Will you listen to your Creator?

Intimacy is part of our deep and desperate human desire to simply belong.

We long to belong because *we were created to belong.*
We crave intimacy because *we were created for intimacy.*
We need to love and be loved because *we were created for love.*
And we were created by love.

*God longs to satisfy my
wildest longings with his fierce love.*

My deepest awareness of myself is
that I am deeply loved by Jesus Christ
and I have done nothing to earn it or
deserve it.

—Brennan Manning

THIRTEEN

COMPASSION, AGAIN AND AGAIN

LORD, if you kept a record of our sins,
who, O Lord, could ever survive?
But you offer forgiveness,
that we might learn to fear you.

Psalm 130:3–4 NLT

The pairing of forgiveness and fear is an unusual one. Is this verse a suggestion that we should be afraid because God knows us so well? No, I believe it is an invitation to tremble in awe and wild wonder of the Most High God, who knows all and yet loves us so well. David models how to maintain a sense of constant wonder by engaging with God's love and endless mercy.

Before Christ, I'd chosen a path of destruction that would have ground every dream and hope I dared to harbor to dust. I still remember the tangible sense of relief I felt that night when I first heard that God actually loved *me*. But the good news did not stop there. I learned that on the cross, Jesus blotted out the record of each and every sin I'd ever committed. I felt immediately lighter. My breathing became deeper and my jaw unclenched. The heavy shroud that sin and shame had layered upon my frame was stripped away and a mantle of Christ's righteousness took its place.

God is *the only one* capable of keeping an exacting record of our sins, and yet he refuses to. Rather than itemize our sins, he plunges any recollection of their taint and violations into oblivion.

> He will again have compassion on us;
>> he will tread our iniquities underfoot.
> You will cast all our sins
>> into the depths of the sea. (Mic. 7:19)

I love the imagery captured in this verse. Out of compassion, he crushes the very things that threaten to crush us. Our evil actions and vices crumble under the weight of his step. And once those idols of sin and shame are ground into unrecognizable fragments, he hurls them into the sea, where they sink to its cold, shadowed depths, never to rise again.

Lovely one, is something weighing you down? Are you ready to let him do this for you? It's time to hand over what you can no longer carry to the One who longs to trample your sin and shame under his feet.

I stand in wild fear and wonder of the One who forgets the very things I have a hard time forgiving myself for.

FOURTEEN

HEIRS OF AN ETERNAL COVENANT

I am God Almighty; walk before me, and be blameless, that I may make my covenant between me and you, and may multiply you greatly.

Genesis 17:1–2

When you discover you are an heir, God will change your title. When God changed Abram's name to Abraham, his life expanded. No longer would he be a man without a nation . . . he would be a father of nations. In Genesis 17, God described in detail what would be the magnitude and reach of this covenant. Abraham's life would be encompassed with words such as *generational* and *everlasting*. The very ground Abraham walked as an outsider and stranger would one day be the inheritance of his offspring and their possession forever. Just as God was with Abraham, he promised to be with Abraham's descendants. I imagine Abraham wept in the presence of God as he glimpsed the goodness of their future.

God tells us he is going to do new and miraculous things in our lives, and yet we waver in unbelief. He says he is about to enlarge our lives, and we tell him there is no need to go to all that trouble . . . *just bless what I have.* What we have and what we do are not vast enough. God wants to get involved. He is thinking generationally.

God in his mercy will even bless what we build in our own strength, but his everlasting covenant is established beyond the realm of human provision.

I have a wild eternal role to play in God's kingdom.

God's destiny for your life is not limited to your current situation.

FIFTEEN

UNRIVALED LORD

> I will give to the LORD the thanks due to his righteousness,
> and I will sing praise to the name of the LORD, the Most High.
>
> Psalm 7:17

When we surrender to all that God is (Lord), our lives are enlarged by his domain. It is hard for us to imagine the use of the word *lord* outside the realm of our experience with human hierarchy. We have known earthly lords who leveraged their positions of power and authority for their own benefit. Throughout human history, renegade lords have used those under their domain. Jesus warned his disciples about this dynamic.

> But Jesus called them to him and said, "You know that the rulers of the Gentiles lord it over them, and their great ones exercise authority over them. It shall not be so among you. But whoever would be great among you must be your servant, and whoever would be first among you must be your slave, even as the Son of Man came not to be served but to serve, and to give his life as a ransom for many." (Matt. 20:25–28)

Every aspect of the life of Jesus served and ransomed. The lordship of Jesus lifts us rather than holds us down.

Our Lord was stripped so that we could be covered.

Jesus was compromised so that we could receive what was promised.

Our Lord was betrayed so that we could be protected.

Jesus was raised from death unto life so that we too could be raised.

Because he is the Lord of all, he is worthy of our all.

As I surrender to my Lord,
my life is wildly enlarged.

SIXTEEN

GUIDED BY THE SPIRIT

God is spirit, and those who worship him must worship in spirit
and truth.

John 4:24

You are a living spirit.

We were all created in the image of God, and God is Spirit. Though it is invisible, this Spirit is as real and as near as our very breath. It is the quickening of God dwelling within us. The Spirit of God animates all that can be touched and gives us the capacity to feel.

God's Spirit speaks life. Don't settle for turning the pages of the Bible without the wind of his Spirit or for religion void of God's presence. The limits of the letter of the law are not simply the humanly impossible legalities of religion—the law also includes what our culture has scribed on our flesh. It is the labels we are encouraged to wear.

Until we see that living by a religion solely based on labels and letters is death—not spirit and life—we will continue to turn to the wrong source for the right thing. We need someone to speak spirit-to-spirit to the depths of our longing and bring clarity to our human confusion.

I don't want the world to define
God for me. I want the Holy
Spirit to reveal God to me.

—A. W. Tozer

SEVENTEEN

THE OFFER
OF TRUTH AND LIFE

I am the way, and the truth, and the life. No one comes to the Father
except through me.

John 14:6

The pursuit of truth is woven deep within us. Without truth, we are like ships without rudders, driven by every wind of doctrine and whim of emotion, which cannot help but drive us to the brink of destruction. As we pursue truth, it will have its way with us. Truth is not a what; it is a Who.

For Jesus's above statement to be true, each element must stand on its own. If Jesus is *the* way and not merely one of *many* ways, then it must be true that no one comes to the Father except through him. If Jesus lied and misrepresented who he was, and is but one of many ways to the Father, then he cannot be the truth. If he is not the truth, it is impossible for Jesus to be the life.

Jesus is absolutely *all* that he says he is or absolutely *none* of it. It is impossible for him to be both. In the words of Benjamin Franklin, "Half a truth is often a great lie." Every partial truth is seeded with a lie.

If Jesus is in fact the way, he must also be the truth and the life. And that impacts the way we live every day.

Jesus, you are my wild, fierce way, truth, and life.

Where I found truth, there found
I my God, who is truth itself.

—Saint Augustine

EIGHTEEN

WHAT DO YOU CALL JESUS?

> Whoever confesses that Jesus is the Son of God, God abides in him, and he in God. So we have come to know and to believe the love that God has for us.
>
> 1 John 4:15–16

ithin this confession, an eternal connection is made, and the gap between his redemption and our reality closes. We are positioned to identify with God based on who he is, not who we are. This means you are who he says you are. The realization and revelation of all the promises that God has positioned you for are intimately tied to what you call Jesus. Do you call Jesus *God*, or do you simply name him Good Teacher?

If you call Jesus Good Teacher, he will instruct you. If you call him Wise Counselor, he will impart wisdom. Separately, these titles are like accepting crumbs instead of a feast. But when Jesus is called on by the name of *Christ*, Son of the *Living God*, then there is a revelation of Jesus the Lord in you.

Because he is love, I am loved and I can love.

Because he is life, I am alive.

Because he is my brother, I am God's daughter.
Because he is almighty, I am mighty.
Because he is wisdom, I am wise.
Because he is, I am.

Jesus Christ, may your image be wildly expressed in me.

Because he is who he is,
I am who he says I am.

NINETEEN

PERFECT LOVE

For our sake he made him to be sin who knew no sin, so that in him
we might become the righteousness of God.

2 Corinthians 5:21

Jesus was loved deeply by his Father, and it's wild that he chose to love us just as deeply as the Father loved him. Jesus loves us in spite of our past. He is not afraid that we will make mistakes in our future. He knows we will. Even though we all make mistakes, that does not mean we are a mistake. Even though we sin, it doesn't mean we are a sin.

No matter how you feel about it, Jesus has made you righteous. The most fearless, loving response you can have to his hopes for you is to honor his faith with an obedient life.

You can spend all your time and energy focused on your sin, and it won't be long until that is all you can see. You will be overwhelmed by your sinfulness, and when it becomes too much, you will turn your gaze to the sinfulness of others.

Jesus does not allow our sins and shadows to shroud his love. When we feel vulnerable, it is the perfect time to lift our gaze in hope rather than avert our eyes in shame. His perfect love opposes all our fears. When I look at myself, I see flaws; when I look to Christ, my imperfections are lost in his radiance.

In Christ, I was made wildly righteous.

Why would I allow my imperfect fears to oppose his flawless love? He set his love on me; therefore, I choose to set my hope on him.

TWENTY

THE REALITY OF GOD

For what can be known about God is plain to them, because God has shown it to them. For his invisible attributes, namely, his eternal power and divine nature, have been clearly perceived, ever since the creation of the world, in the things that have been made. So they are without excuse.

Romans 1:19–20

reation declares the reality of our great God. It reveals a God of wonder and boundless creativity. If no one ever told us there was a Creator, the symphony of nature would draw our eyes and ears to his existence. All that is made reveals the One without a maker. Everything we see declares his existence, and all that we know reveals the reality of the unknown. Our God alone is supreme. He alone is the Lord thy God, the One above all. The Psalms paint such magnificent descriptions of the God Most High:

> For GOD is great, and worth a thousand Hallelujahs.
> His furious beauty puts the other gods to shame;
> Pagan gods are mere tatters and rags.

God made the heavens—

Royal splendor radiates from him,

A powerful beauty sets him apart. (Ps. 96:4–6 Message)

It is impossible to read these verses and somehow miss the awe of our God.

Creation declares the wild wonder of the One.

It's not great faith you need; it is faith in a great God.

—N. T. Wright

TWENTY-ONE

HOLY GOD, HOLY DAUGHTER

His divine power has granted to us all things that pertain to life and godliness, through the knowledge of him who called us to his own glory and excellence, by which he has granted to us his precious and very great promises, so that through them you may become partakers of the divine nature, having escaped from the corruption that is in the world because of sinful desire.

2 Peter 1:3–4

God's divine power has graced us with *all* that we need for this wild life. Nothing we could possibly need went missing along the way. We have been equipped with *everything* we need to practice holiness. God is holy in grace, holy in power, holy in faith, holy in love, holy in truth, holy in knowledge, and holy in judgment. Our God always was holy, is now holy, and will always be holy. And he invites us, who have not been holy, who are not even now acting holy, to be holy. This is not about attempting and failing at human goodness. Because we are his own, we've been granted the divine privilege of partaking of his holy nature.

Jesus expressed the holiness of the Father. When it comes to holiness, Jesus is both our pattern and our High Priest. Because he and God are one, Jesus did and said only what he heard and saw his holy Father say and do. And that is the pattern for our lives as well.

> *The Holy God has equipped me with everything I need to live a holy life.*

Because God is holy in all he is, he is holy in all he does.

TWENTY-TWO

HOLY FEAR

In that day he will be your sure foundation,
    providing a rich store of salvation, wisdom, and knowledge.
    The fear of the LORD will be your treasure.

Isaiah 33:6 NLT

Just as God is constant in love, he is constant in mercy. He swears by his unchanging nature rather than our changeable one. In Psalm 103:17, we read how his love is promised to those who fear him. God is not looking for perfection because, outside of Christ, there are no sinless people! But he *is* looking for those who fear him. Why? What does it mean to fear God in our day of familiarity and irreverence?

One way to fear the Lord is to depart from evil. In Proverbs 3:7, we read, "Be not wise in your own eyes; fear the LORD, and turn away from evil." The Passion Translation says it this way: "For wisdom comes when you adore him with undivided devotion and avoid everything that's wrong."

When we combine the meanings found in these two interpretations of the same verse, we conclude that as we look to him in awe and cultivate a wild wonder, we turn from everything that is evil and wrong. And the wonder of the unchanging One changes us.

*I turn from evil and run
toward the wild goodness of God.*

The remarkable thing about God is that when you fear God, you fear nothing else, whereas if you do not fear God, you fear everything else.

—Oswald Chambers

TWENTY-THREE

CONSTANT FOR OUR CHANGE

God is not man, that he should lie,

   or a son of man, that he should change his mind.

Has he said, and will he not do it?

   Or has he spoken, and will he not fulfill it?

Numbers 23:19

*G*od doesn't change. He doesn't need to change. He responds to us based on who he is rather than who we are or are not.

And God does not change his mind. His heart is set on you. He will do what he said he would. What he speaks will be fully realized. Things may look different or arrive later than you expect, but you can rest assured in this: If your Father has said it . . . it will happen.

God is our immovable mountain, the constant Rock that is higher so that we can lift our eyes, knowing he is always there. Because he is constant, his Word and his ways are consistent with each other. He cannot say one thing and then act in another manner. He is unified in all his expressions.

The very fact that God doesn't change should give us the courage to believe that we can! He is consistently good and faithful. Even though our Lord doesn't change, he is determined to remake us. Because we know what to expect with God, we can have the confidence and freedom to grow into all we were meant to be.

> *I can change because the One who loves me never changes.*

God does not change.

TWENTY-FOUR

GOD ABOVE ALL

> You shall not make idols for yourselves or erect an image or pillar, and you shall not set up a figured stone in your land to bow down to it, for I am the LORD your God.
>
> Leviticus 26:1

Most of us have not erected pillars or figures of stone in our houses, but that does not mean we are not carrying idols in our hearts. *An idol is anything that you give your strength to or draw your strength from.* It is where you go to get your life. It could be what you run to as a refuge. This could be something as mundane as food or something as far-reaching as your involvement with social media.

For some of us, our feelings are an idol. If we *feel* beautiful, we believe we are beautiful. If we *feel* good, we believe we are good. If we live by our feelings alone, they will lie to us, and it will not be long before we are led astray.

The truth is, you are beautiful because our God beautifies the meek with salvation (Ps. 149:4). You are beautiful because God makes all things beautiful in their time (Eccles. 3:11).

God is our strength, life, refuge, and our truth. No person, relationship, feeling, or thing is to have power over you—nothing except God.

Do not allow the foolish idols and image-makers of what this world calls beauty speak into and dictate your life when God has already spoken blessing over it!

> *Because I am fiercely loved, I refuse to allow my feelings to be an idol.*

An idol is anything that you give your strength to or draw your strength from.

TWENTY-FIVE

NEW CREATION

> Since you have heard about Jesus and have learned the truth that comes from him, throw off your old sinful nature and your former way of life, which is corrupted by lust and deception. Instead, let the Spirit renew your thoughts and attitudes. Put on your new nature, created to be like God—truly righteous and holy.
>
> Ephesians 4:21–24 NLT

Throw it off! The Holy Spirit of grace empowers us to remove our former fallen nature and filthy shrouds of self-righteousness as though they were death shrouds. (Because they are!) Why would anyone want to put a new garment over a filthy old one? Sooner or later, the stain and the stink of the soiled garment would seep through and mar the new one. And none of us can bear the weight of wearing both. When we come under Christ's lordship, we put away our shameful, self-willed practices and walk as children of light. We cast off the old nature with its old patterns as we renew our minds and attitudes toward the godly and the holy.

Once we *know* better, we *do* better.

Once we *know* the truth (Jesus), we are empowered to *do* the truth.

Lust no longer has the right to distort our longings. Greed and the deceitfulness of riches no longer have the right to veil our minds. Rather than call the old new, we renew.

I am renewed by his wild, fierce love.

Once we *know* better,
we *do* better.

TWENTY-SIX

CLOTHED IN FORGIVENESS

If we confess our sins, he is faithful and just and will forgive us our sins and purify us from all unrighteousness.

1 John 1:9 NIV

Shame is never something that we are, but there are times when shame is something that we feel. There are times when our actions can only be called shameful. I have behaved in ways that were shameful. This doesn't make me shameful. This means I've said and done things that I'm ashamed of. When we allow shame to cause us to turn away from God, we attempt to cover ourselves with fig leaves and, in turn, blame those around us. We can choose to allow shame to separate us from God, or we can choose to turn from the darkness and allow his light and love to bond us in a deeper manner to our Creator.

In the light of his love and holiness, God ultimately removes our shame.

My shame was not removed by making excuses for my poor behavior and sin. I cannot look back and call my shameful practices honorable in light of my circumstances. My shame was removed when I turned away from a life of lies and chose to live in truth.

Transformation does not lie and deny our nakedness.

It does not call the naked clothed.

It does not hide from the presence of God behind justifications and excuses.

Transformation begins as we admit our nakedness.

It confesses our failed attempts to try to cover ourselves in temporal trappings and the fig leaves of earth.

It admits that these never actually covered us.

It lays aside all vain human attempts and asks our holy Father to clothe us in truth and cover us in his forgiveness and love.

I turn from shame and embrace
his wild, transforming truth.

TWENTY-SEVEN

SEEK THE LIGHT

You have become spiritual adulterers who are having an affair, an unholy relationship with the world. Don't you know that flirting with the world's values places you at odds with God? Whoever chooses to be the world's friend makes himself God's enemy!

Does the Scripture mean nothing to you that says, "The Spirit that God breathed into our hearts is a jealous Lover who intensely desires to have more and more of us"?

James 4:4–5 TPT

There are those who would argue that this impassioned plea of the apostle James, the brother of Jesus, is not for us today. They reason that we have evolved to a higher place. And yet, when I look around, I can't remember a time when I have seen humanity sunk so low.

When we are afraid of exposure, it is easier to choose to love our darkness and blame the light for its exposing tendencies. The Holy Spirit can light our way and counsel us along our paths. The only way to tackle our fear of being called out is to invite the light into every area of our lives. When we decide to hate everything that shadows the soul by embracing the light, we will work to remove the darkness it reveals.

Love flourishes in an undivided heart; therefore, God hates what divides our affections. The early church understood this. Heaven has a very different value system than this earth's. Therefore, we are warned against even flirting with the world's values and encouraged to seek the light.

> *Because I am fiercely loved,*
> *I invite God's light into every area of my life.*

TWENTY-EIGHT

IN CHRIST

In him we have obtained an inheritance, having been predestined according to the purpose of him who works all things according to the counsel of his will.

Ephesians 1:11

*L*ovely one, hear me. You do not inhabit a hollowed-out hole in Christ, chiseled out sparingly to make room for you. In Christ, who unifies all things in heaven and on earth (Eph. 1:10), you have access to the whole. You are not an intruder. You are not a guest. You are family. Actually, *family* isn't intimate enough. You are one within Jesus even as he is one within the Father. You are part of the all in all.

Both provision and a place have been prepared for you. This abundance includes all the fruit of the Spirit, our gifting in the Spirit, and peace, righteousness, and joy.

Once we possess the knowledge of this love, why would any of us even think of eyeing the suitors of this earthly realm? The prince of the power of the air has no love for us. But we are no longer subjects of his realm. We are the beloved of Christ and citizens of his kingdom.

We know that every good and true gift comes from our Father. Let's set our hearts on things above, where they will not be corrupted or stolen from us. Let's keep our hearts and treasure in the right place.

As his fiercely loved daughter,
I am one with Christ.

You become dangerous to the Enemy
when you are fully awake to God.

TWENTY-NINE

ASCEND

"Come,

    let's climb GOD's Mountain,

    go to the House of the God of Jacob.

    He'll show us the way he works

       so we can live the way we're made."

Zion's the source of the revelation.

    GOD's Message comes from Jerusalem.

Isaiah 2:2–3 Message,

emphasis added

*D*are to embrace this wild invitation to go higher. Dare to believe that God is not distant or disapproving; he is near, and he loves you more than you know. There are things immersed in the deep waters of your life that you can no longer see but that he longs to uncover.

Our Father is our example. Just as Jesus did only what he saw his Father doing, we are invited into the landscape of God's wild rescue of us all. God will show us the way he works so we can live the way we're made. We were made for immovable, invincible intimacy that will not be dissuaded by our deepest longings or put off by our most primal fears. If we ask, he will show us the light of his goodness. Pause, ponder, and allow his light to quicken you.

Receive what your Creator speaks into your life. Let him release his light in your heart and soul and remove any darkness and confusion there. Embrace your designation of daughter. And pray, "Show me the way you are working in my life so I can live the way I was made: for your glory. In the name of Jesus, amen."

As I draw near, may I see how you work and, in seeing, learn to surrender.

THIRTY

UNFAILING LOVE

"For the mountains may depart
   and the hills be removed,
but *my steadfast love shall not depart from you,*
   and my covenant of peace shall not be removed,"
says the LORD, who has compassion on you.

Isaiah 54:10, emphasis added

The flame of God's love does not flicker in the wind of our waywardness. His love remains when we are irresponsible, unresponsive, and rebellious. He cannot bless these actions, but even in the midst of them, his kindness leads us to repentance and his love does not falter.

His affection toward us does not vary according to our behavior. We cannot earn what we never deserved any more than we can pay for what has been freely given.

People may come and go, but his unconditional love will remain. Because his love is immovable, we have been wrapped in a covenant of peace. From his realm of highest power, he whispers peace to every storm in our bodies and to every tempest that assaults our minds. His compassion for us knows no bounds. We can be at peace because there is no denying his love for us. To deny his love for us, God would have to deny his love for his Son.

Because of his unchanging love for you, you were redeemed in Christ. You may ask, "How can I be sure this is true?" His love for us can be seen: "But God shows his love for us in that while we were still sinners, Christ died for us" (Rom. 5:8).

I trust in God's fierce, wild, unfailing love.

His love *for* us is not dependent *on* us.

THIRTY-ONE

SPIRIT-FILLED LIFE

The Spirit of God has made me,
and the breath of the Almighty gives me life.

Job 33:4

ou were made for personal, spirit-filled connection with the Father. In the fall, this intimate weaving of the soul and spirit was rent. This could be likened to a vessel that is no longer full. Even though it is his breath that sustains our frame, we carry an awareness of our gap, our void. We breathe because he is, but the shallowness of each breath says there is more because it doesn't fill us. Without *God's* Spirit, we live as those who are on life support.

Just like in the creation story, the Spirit of God hovers over your life with gentle and careful purpose. He wants to

- quicken you with his light (2 Cor. 4:6)
- separate light from darkness (2 Cor. 6:14)
- create a canopy of expanse over your life (Rom. 4:7–8)

- roll back the dark blanket of water and reveal the new ground (Heb. 11:29)
- release the seeds buried within your soil so they may sprout and bring forth fruit (Mark 4:20)
- call forth life and wonder in your deep waters (John 7:38)
- free your heart from fear so it can take flight in faith (Mark 6:50)
- astound you with the creativity of his vast creation (Ps. 19:1–6)
- breathe life, his life, into the cavity created by sin, reweave your spirit and soul, and heal all that has been rent (John 20:21–22; Col. 2:2)

Because I am fiercely loved,
I embrace the Holy Spirit's
wild work in my life.

THIRTY-TWO

LOVE WITHOUT END

By his divine power, God has given us everything we need for living a godly life. We have received all of this by coming to know him, the one who called us to himself by means of his marvelous glory and excellence.

2 Peter 1:3 NLT

Let's look at this verse again from another angle. You and I were born of the Spirit, sealed with the Spirit, indwelled by the Spirit, baptized in the Spirit, made one in the Spirit, given gifts by the Spirit, and commissioned into ministry by the Spirit. Everything we need has been provided by our God, who loves us without end.

This is the very reason the apostle Paul assured each of us of the following: "I'm writing this letter to all the devoted believers who have been made holy by being one with Jesus, the Anointed One. May God himself, the heavenly Father of our Lord Jesus Christ, release grace over you and impart total well-being into your lives" (Eph. 1:2 TPT).

Do you see our heavenly Father's intimate involvement in this process? We say yes to a life of devoted belief by pledging our hearts. In turn, God graces us to receive the fullness of his divine impartation into our lives.

No blessing that heaven has to offer has been left out or withheld. The extravagant provision for God's bride is in step with the extravagance of his love for her. And you are part of the bride of Christ. "Blessed be the God and Father of our Lord Jesus Christ, who has blessed us in Christ with *every spiritual blessing in the heavenly places*" (Eph. 1:3, emphasis added).

In Christ, I am divinely blessed and sealed.

THIRTY-THREE

DRAWING FROM OUR WELL

For my people have done two evil things: They have abandoned me—the fountain of living water. And they have dug for themselves cracked cisterns that can hold no water at all!

Jeremiah 2:13 NLT

There is a very real well within each of us: our soul. It is that space of God-longing that Jeremiah calls a cistern. Our soul-wells can range from very shallow to very deep. But it doesn't matter how deep a well is . . . if the cistern is cracked, it will not hold water. A well can be deepened as well as strengthened and reinforced.

Sometimes the water of the well of my soul feels stagnant. Other times, I can actually sense its flow. But the water is always there whether the well is trickling, half full, or overflowing. In ancient days, enemies would fill wells with dirt because they understood water was the source of life. Rough patches in life can do the same.

If you feel like your well has been overwhelmed, you can open it up by giving voice to your deepest sorrows or the longings of your soul. When I feel murky, muddy, or possibly even mean, sometimes all it takes is a song to open my well and refresh my soul. Laughing and spending time with family and godly friends fills the cistern. Reading the Word, keeping a journal, and praying refresh me like a long drink from a cool fountain on a hot day.

I fill my soul with living water.

Spring up, O well!

—Numbers 21:17

THIRTY-FOUR

DEAR WOMAN

Believe me, dear woman, the time has come when you will worship the Father neither on a mountain nor in Jerusalem, but in your heart.

John 4:21 TPT

The Samaritan woman at the well, also known as Photina, had suffered hardships that led her to living as a shamed outcast. In her conversation with Jesus, she recognizes him as a prophet, one who speaks the words of God. She honors Jesus as the prophet he truly is, and in return, Jesus calls forth what she truly is: *dear.*

This term means "beloved and cherished, prized, precious and priceless, valued and treasured." I have to wonder when she had last been called by any term of endearment. He was rebuilding her broken heart and wounded spirit with words of destiny.

Even now, I hear Jesus inviting each and every one of his daughters: "Believe me, my valued, treasured, and loved woman, your time has come . . ." Your time to believe is now. Pause a moment. What has he whispered to your soul?

Our God is not closest to you on a mountain, in a city, or even at a church. No individual can keep you from his presence. Thankfully, no mistake can separate you from what abides within you. Jesus awaits your worship at the well of your heart. The Scriptures remind us that our God is as close as a whisper: "But what does it say? 'The word is near you, in your mouth and in your heart'" (Rom. 10:8).

I can worship and experience Jesus's presence wherever I am.

THIRTY-FIVE

A SECURE FAITH

Each time he said, "My grace is all you need. My power works best in weakness." So now I am glad to boast about my weaknesses, so that the power of Christ can work through me.

2 Corinthians 12:9 NLT

*O*ur position and faith in Christ are not based on our ability to hold on. The moment we hide ourselves in him, we are secured in his ability to hold us. In Christ, our Rock, our unchanging refuge, our hiding place, we are safe. When we fall and fail, we fall in him, never outside of his eternal reach.

In order that we might abide *in him*, God places a measure of his faith *in us*. We stumble when we place our faith in others. We will never falter when our faith is in God. Let the faith of God have entrance in your life. Invite it in. You have tried and failed in your own strength. You have watched others falter as they attempted to climb the scree-strewn rock of faith in the strength of self. Just because faith is unseen doesn't mean it doesn't exist or won't happen. Faith is the hidden quickening of hope that leaps within us to help us believe there can be more. Faith gives us the courage to ask for more, to dare to dream that in Christ we too can be resolute, immovable, and invincible.

Because I am fiercely loved,
I am held firm in his wild embrace.

When we fall and fail,
we fall in him.

THIRTY-SIX

TRUTH IN LOVE

Having purified your souls by your obedience to the truth for a sincere brotherly love, love one another earnestly from a pure heart.

1 Peter 1:22

bedience to truth purifies our souls. This purification happens through doing, not merely hearing. We are saved through Jesus's sacrifice, and our minds are renewed by the Word, and our souls are purified through obedience to truth. It is a journey.

As we obey truth, our hearts are refined so that we can love one another deeply. Love cannot go deeper than the room the heart makes for it. Abiding in God's Word increases our depth and capacity to truly love. A heart that resists truth can love only superficially. Christ is the imperishable seed and our adamant Cornerstone of all truth. Outside of truth, love is impossible.

A pursuit of holiness is not even possible outside of God's Word. This pursuit is not subject to our interpretation. When the Word has its way in us, we love, and we produce fruit that remains because it is holy and true. There will be times when obedience to truth will feel like a death in this world. But remember, friends, our days on earth are but a vapor. We will wake to discover our true lives in the next.

Holiness is our connection with an eternal perspective.

Holiness is our otherworldliness.

These verses return us to the Cornerstone and what it means to be part of the living Stone and a holy people.

*The Word of God renews my capacity
for holiness and truth.*

Our minds are renewed by obedience
to the truth of God's Word.

THIRTY-SEVEN

TRUTH EVIDENT

If we claim that we share life with him, but keep walking in the realm of darkness, we're fooling ourselves and not living the truth. But if we keep living in the pure light that surrounds him, we share *unbroken* fellowship with one another, and the blood of Jesus, his Son, continually cleanses us from all sin.

1 John 1:6–7 TPT

As God puts his hand on us, it is evidenced in our lives. When the Word of God is not only preached with boldness but also lived with confidence, there is an atmosphere for change. There is a shift. We don't just hear truth . . . we live truth. As the Holy Spirit quickens us, we come to attention, stand straighter, and have a greater awareness that the truth we carry within us is sacred. When God's Word is preached through our lives, the Holy Spirit puts steel in our convictions.

Those who have ears to hear will likewise receive the wisdom and courage to live in truth. The Word of God falls on good soil and produces a harvest first and foremost in our lives. This happens first *in* us so it can happen next *through* us.

If we don't know the truth, we are invited to seek it. We seek it in God's Word and see it in the life of Jesus. And once it's discovered, we cannot continue to close our ears to the deafening cry for truth in a culture captive to lies. Even now, people are discovering that what they thought was freedom is in fact chains. Jesus is our truth in a world of lies.

We oppose the degradation of truth when we live the Word of truth. We cannot choose to remain in a posture of quiet comfort when so many are living in the discomfort of lies. Through him, we have the strength to live the courage of our convictions and live every aspect of our lives as an expression of his truth in love.

His Word is truth.

THIRTY-EIGHT

LIVE THE TRUTH

So Jesus said to the Jews who had believed him, "If you abide in my word, you are truly my disciples, and you will know the truth, and the truth will set you free."

John 8:31–32

As we live in the truth (God's Word), we will come to intimately know the truth, and the truth that we live will set us free. Living in truth breaks the bonds of captivity just as surely as living in lies binds us. Jesus invites us to truth in the same way that all were invited to the wedding feast.

"Go therefore to the main roads and invite to the wedding feast as many as you find." And those servants went out into the roads and gathered all whom they found, both bad and good. So the wedding hall was filled with guests.

But when the king came in to look at the guests, he saw there a man who had no wedding garment. And he said to him, "Friend, how did you get in here without a wedding garment?" And he was speechless. Then the king said to the attendants, "Bind him hand and foot and cast him into the

outer darkness. In that place there will be weeping and gnashing of teeth."
For many are called, but few are chosen. (Matt. 22:9–14)

All are called, but not all choose to embrace the covering that was provided for them, just as everyone is invited to live in truth, but not everything is truth. Jesus is the truth. The Lamb is our wedding garment. We are invited to clothe ourselves in Christ and his righteousness rather than try to slip in wearing our own unrighteous rags.

Because I am fiercely loved,
I clothe myself in Christ.

THIRTY-NINE

LISTEN TO THE WIND WORDS

So train your heart to listen when I speak
and open your spirit wide to expand your discernment.

Proverbs 2:2 TPT

ecause we have the Bible in our possession, should we only read and cease to listen? I believe the ethereal question raised seven times in the book of Revelation alone remains as an invitation to us all to hear today:

Are your ears awake? Listen. Listen to the Wind Words, the Spirit blowing through the churches. (Rev 2:7, 11, 17, 29; 3:6, 13, 22 Message)

This sevenfold repetition cannot help but underscore its urgent plea with us all. It also highlights the realization that I can be awake even while my ears remain asleep. These are days that require both discernment and Scripture. The letter without the Spirit leads us down a pathway to law, and the Spirit without knowledge of the Word can lead us to weird. We need both.

We need to hear the voice of God. Rarely is this voice audible. It often comes as a whispered prompting in your heart. Perhaps it will compel you to read a passage of Scripture, call a friend, or give to someone in need. I want to assure you that God will never speak something that is contrary to his Word. *The Holy Spirit animates what God's Word outlines.*

What might happen if we invite the Holy Spirit to speak into the very places of our lives where we declared him silent? Will you let him speak to you one-on-one?

Holy Spirit, awaken my ears to hear your wild words.

FORTY

ALL WE DO

> If I give away all I have, and if I deliver up my body to be burned,
> but have not love, I gain nothing. . . . So now faith, hope, and love
> abide, these three; but the greatest of these is love.
>
> 1 Corinthians 13:3, 13

In 1 Corinthians 13:3, Paul lists acts of unmitigated generosity, such as giving away *all* our possessions to the poor and the unthinkable act of submitting our bodies to the flames of agonizing martyrdom, and tells the church that if such acts are not motivated by love, they will add nothing to the giver. He is driving his point home:

$$\text{Everything} - \text{Love} = \text{Nothing}$$

Without love, we are nothing.

Without love, we add nothing.

Having received such a generous love from our Father, we are to love as we are loved:

Fearlessly, because there is no fear in love.

Selflessly, because love is not selfish.

Free of offense, because love is not easily offended.

Triumphantly, because love never fails.

Endlessly, because love is eternal.

God insists that love be the motive behind all we do.

This is a sobering picture. In all honesty, only eternity will accurately weigh our motives in this matter. I readily admit that my own life may have an alarming heap of words and deeds void of eternal value. There is no reason you should not learn from my mistakes. Like so much treasure that is consumed by the catalytic heat of fire, your works will one day be refined by the intense light of God's presence as your motives are revealed.

Because I am fiercely loved,
love is my motivation.

FORTY-ONE

AS WE ARE LOVED

> And hope does not put us to shame, because God's love has been poured into our hearts through the Holy Spirit who has been given to us.
>
> Romans 5:5

The following passage from Romans is a brilliant outline of how to love others. Let's love, with God's help, as we are loved.

Let's turn this Scripture into our prayer by asking the Holy Spirit to show us the places where our hearts need to be unlocked.

Dear heavenly Father, I want to love how you love. I choose to . . .

Love one another with brotherly affection. Outdo one another in showing honor. Do not be slothful in zeal, be fervent in spirit, serve the Lord. Rejoice in hope, be patient in tribulation, be constant in prayer. Contribute to the needs of the saints and seek to show hospitality.

Bless those who persecute you; bless and do not curse them. Rejoice with those who rejoice, weep with those who weep. Live in harmony with one another. Do not be haughty, but associate with the lowly. Never be wise in your own sight. Repay no one evil for evil, but give thought to do what is honorable in the sight of all. If possible, so far as it depends on you, live peaceably with all. Beloved, never avenge yourselves, but leave it to the wrath of God, for it is written, "Vengeance is mine, I will repay, says the Lord." To the contrary, "if your enemy is hungry, feed him; if he is thirsty, give him something to drink; for by so doing you will heap burning coals on his head." Do not be overcome by evil, but overcome evil with good (Rom. 12:10–21).

Because I am fiercely loved,
I love others fiercely.

FORTY-TWO

LOVE LIFTS OTHERS

> Now he was teaching in one of the synagogues on the Sabbath. And
> behold, there was a woman who had had a disabling spirit for eigh-
> teen years. She was bent over and could not fully straighten herself.
> When Jesus saw her, he called her over and said to her, "Woman,
> you are freed from your disability."
>
> Luke 13:10–12

For eighteen long, oppressive years, a disabling spirit had reduced the posture of this woman. Maybe this woman had been told to try harder, to pray longer, to repent of sin. She felt the shame. When Love saw her, he called her out, spoke freedom and release, and then touched her. Sadly, not everyone shared her joy.

But the ruler of the synagogue, indignant because Jesus had healed on the Sabbath, said to the people, "There are six days in which work ought to be done. Come on those days and be healed, and not on the Sabbath day." (v. 14)

The release of this daughter stepped squarely on some religious toes. But the heart of God was moved to action because God is adamant about freeing his captive children.

Sadly, there are times when it is difficult to love religion and people at the same time. If you find yourself at this crossroads, choose to love people rather than the dogma of doctrine. Love has the ability to conquer lies and overcome deception, but hating and judging people will push them away. Faith works by love. There are times when love means telling the truth and other times when love means being the truth. Jesus did both. By freeing this daughter, Jesus exemplified God's love for people over religious policy or practice.

> *The wild, unconditional love of Jesus*
> *supersedes the judgment of religion.*

FORTY-THREE

LOVE IN ACTION

If anyone boasts, "I love God," and goes right on hating his brother or sister, thinking nothing of it, he is a liar. If he won't love the person he can see, how can he love the God he can't see? The command we have from Christ is blunt: Loving God includes loving people. You've got to love both.

1 John 4:20–21 Message

We can know about love without being loving, just as we can embrace the concept of love without embracing people.

We are called to love *everyone*. We cannot choose to love just those who look and act like us. We must love those who disagree with us. This does not mean we compromise our beliefs or confuse others with our actions. Somehow our culture has equated loving with approving. There are times when the most loving thing we can do is lovingly disagree. This is the tightrope of our day. We must daily choose to live with a sensitive awareness of other people.

Rather than being defined, love should be demonstrated. It is not hard to recognize love when we see it. Love is not a feeling; it is a way of life. In many ways, love is the greatest habit that any of us could develop.

Love fulfills the law. Love frees us of all emotional, physical, and social debts. We owe only what we have been so freely given . . . love.

Love moves us to action.

And because God loves people, he never wants our freedom to hinder his love from reaching them. Love makes us mindful of how our actions, words, and choices affect others.

Because I am fiercely loved,
I am mindful of loving everyone.

FORTY-FOUR

FOR HIS GLORY

> But I say, love your enemies! Pray for those who persecute you! In
> that way, you will be acting as true children of your Father in heaven.
>
> Matthew 5:44–45 NLT

You have complete control over how you choose to see others. All you have to do is remember these two key things about control:

1. You can't control, and you are not responsible for, what others say, think, do, or feel.
2. You can control, and you are responsible for, what *you* say, think, do, or feel.

We all know what enemies and rivals can do *to* us, but have you considered what they can do *for* us?

Rivals and enemies reveal God's power. How do the obstacles and conflicts in your life reveal how God is releasing you from oppression or readying you for the future?

Rivals reveal your destiny. They have the power to pull you out of obscurity or knock you out of your place of prominence. The good news is that you get to choose what they will produce in your life. Will your rival best you . . . or bring out the best in you?

You are filled with the same Spirit that raised Christ from the grave. This means you will have a wild, unexpected response to a rival. Rivals want you to fight on their terms and in your own strength. You must be bigger than that. As a child of the God who has no rival, you can do good when you are dealt evil and respond with love when you are treated with hate. You can be a wise steward of what *you* control rather than reacting to things outside of your control. And remember that, ultimately, self-control is a fruit of the Spirit that we would all do well to develop.

I fight evil with good.

FORTY-FIVE

SECURE IN GOD'S LOVE

> For I am sure that neither death nor life, nor angels nor rulers, nor things present nor things to come, nor powers, nor height nor depth, nor anything else in all creation, will be able to separate us from the love of God in Christ Jesus our Lord.
>
> Romans 8:38–39

Nothing can separate you from the invincible love of Christ. There is no who, there is no what. His love cannot be taken, for we have been placed in Christ. The cruelty of conflict and the dangers of war can never make him side against us. There is no disaster large enough to unseat the love of our Prince of Peace. His love is more certain than death and more real than life. His love for us supersedes the domains of both the angelic and the demonic realms. There is nothing that has been, is, or will be in the entire span of creation that will ever have the capacity to divorce us from the love of God in Christ Jesus our Lord. His love for you is as adamant as his love for Jesus. This means that God would have to reject his Son to reject you.

*I am never separated
from God's fierce love.*

Never again imagine there is a
place or circumstance in which
you are alone.

FORTY-SIX

THE BETTER INSTRUCTOR

When troubles of any kind come your way, consider it an opportunity for great joy. For you know that when your faith is tested, your endurance has a chance to grow.

James 1:2–3 NLT

pposition comes at us from all kinds of angles. I've learned that when I'm discouraged, that is a good time to remember the faithfulness of God. He carried me each and every time I didn't think I could go on another day. I have learned more about the faithfulness of God from my enemies than from my friends. I will go even further: I have learned more about myself from my enemies than from my friends.

Friends will offer you shelter, which is a good thing but not necessarily a dynamic that fosters growth. Friends want to see you protected from the storms of life, while an enemy will do their best to lock you out in the pouring rain. But what if you are in a season when God wants you to learn that he is your ultimate shelter? Who is a better instructor: a rival or a friend?

Rivals are a fact of life. And yet rivals are not without purpose. Creating a life without rival is not about removing rivals from your life. Rather, it is about understanding that truly all things can work together for our good when we are called according to God's purpose. We can use the dynamics of rivalry to spur us on to greater growth and insight.

Because I am fiercely loved,
I know God has a purpose in opposition.

A certain amount of opposition is a great help to a man. Kites rise against, not with, the wind.

—Lewis Mumford

FORTY-SEVEN

ALL UNIQUE

Don't, by the way, read too much into the differences here between men and women. Neither man nor woman can go it alone or claim priority.

1 Corinthians 11:10 Message

*I*n Christ, men and women are interdependent rather than independent, yet there still exists in Christian culture the age-old rivalry known as the battle of the sexes.

The differences of men and women were meant to complement one another. Where there is mutual dependence and inclusion, supremacy and hierarchy are eliminated.

The apostle Paul continues, "Man was created first, as a beautiful shining reflection of God—that is true. But the head on a woman's body clearly outshines in beauty the head of her 'head,' her husband" (v. 11 Message). I love the value Paul bestows on men and women, husbands and wives.

"The first woman came from man, true—but ever since then, every man comes from a woman! And since virtually everything comes from

God anyway, let's quit going through these 'who's first' routines" (v. 12 Message).

The rivalry of who is first and who is best should come to a screeching halt with the revelation of who God is. We need to recover our divine perspective that God alone is holy. He is first and last, our Alpha and Omega. No one loves and leads like our Father. This means he does not love sons more and daughters less. Nor does he love each gender equally. He loves male and female uniquely. When we elevate one above the other, we deviate from God's idea.

Because God loves his daughters uniquely,
I don't need to be part of gender wars.

FORTY-EIGHT

A SHIFT IN PERSPECTIVE

Dear friends, don't be surprised at the fiery trials you are going through, as if something strange were happening to you. Instead, be very glad—for these trials make you partners with Christ in his suffering, so that you will have the wonderful joy of seeing his glory when it is revealed to all the world.

1 Peter 4:12–13 NLT

When you find yourself involved in a senseless rivalry, your heart feels assaulted. You are bombarded with questions that cause you to second-guess yourself and your motives. You wonder, *Is there something wrong with me? God, where are you? How did this happen? Why does this keep on happening?*

Often, the only answer we receive to these questions is silence. We begin to question whether God hears us. I have come to learn that God is quiet when there is an intermission. The scene is about to change, and the characters are finding their places on set. Be encouraged. Your season is about to transition. Rather than measuring yourself by where you are, remember what he has already brought you through.

As we listen in silence, we are poised for a transition. Will we believe what God has said, or will we heed what our rival accusers are saying? The same God who began this good work in us will be faithful to complete it. Will we allow the attacks to harden our hearts, or will we allow God to heal us? Will we focus our attention on the words of an enemy or on the words of our Creator?

So often, it is our rival that reveals our true thoughts and feelings, our true self. We can argue our case, our position, our opinion, or we can lay it before God. We can thank God that he is using a rival to refine and reposition us, or we can whine. We can complain, or we can pray and sing. The choice will always be ours to make.

In seasons of hardship, I will turn to you.

FORTY-NINE

RISE AGAIN

For the righteous falls seven times and rises again,
but the wicked stumble in times of calamity.

Proverbs 24:16

A portion of *The Paradoxical Commandments* by Kent M. Keith reads,

People are illogical, unreasonable, and self-centered.
Love them anyway.

The good you do today will be forgotten tomorrow.
Do good anyway.

Give the world the best you have and you'll get kicked in the teeth.
*Give the world the best you have anyway.**

Both the righteous and the wicked trip, falter, and fall. The only difference is that love compels the righteous to get back up. The wicked stay down and

---

* Kent M. Keith, *The Paradoxical Commandments* (Makawao, HI: Inner Ocean, 2001).

often attempt to pull others down alongside them, but the righteous rise up, lift others, and press on. Love always chooses to rise again.

God always believes better things of me than I believe of myself. He doesn't resign me to my past, because he holds my future. He draws me out of my cowardice and fear to bring out his best in me. We can do the same for others.

> Rather, *speaking the truth in love*, we are to grow up in every way into him who is the head, into Christ, from whom the whole body, joined and held together by every joint with which it is equipped, when each part is working properly, makes the body grow so that it builds itself up in love. (Eph. 4:15–16, emphasis added)

People will disappoint us. Things will happen that will challenge the goodness we work for. Love builds the body. Hateful words, fear, and bitterness cause decay. And yet love is stronger than hate and fear. Love always chooses to rise again.

I choose to be resilient and rise in love.

FIFTY

LOVE WITHOUT RIVAL

A new commandment I give to you, that you love one another: just as
I have loved you, you also are to love one another. By this all people
will know that you are my disciples, if you have love for one another.

John 13:34–35

Love can feel like opening ourselves up to the potential of being
hurt or betrayed. But when you really think about it, how can
love put us at risk when love cannot fail? Love has the power to
heal whatever life wounds.

There are many ways to love courageously.

Boldly loving your spouse is one way. Children and parents should
be loved fearlessly. Our friendships should be nurtured with love rather
than diminished by jealousy, possessiveness, and fear. You can love what
you do and where you work. You may love being part of an organization
or a church. You can love reading and laughing. Regardless of where
you find love, sooner or later you will likewise find challenges and even
disappointments.

Which brings up the next act of courageous love: loving your enemies. Why would Jesus ask us to do such a wild, crazy thing?

Because this is the kind of love that separates the sheep from the goats. We are distinguished when we love those who wish us harm. When you *choose* to love the ones who would bind and injure you, something shifts. Even if your circumstances don't change, you are no longer trapped; you are free.

Fear reacts. Love chooses.

Fear is bondage. Love is freedom.

I choose love and freedom.

FIFTY-ONE

FAITHFUL LOVE, FEARLESS LOVE

> Love never gives up, never loses faith, is always hopeful, and endures
> through every circumstance.
>
> 1 Corinthians 13:7 NLT

earless love is based not on the performance of a person but on the loving faithfulness of God. It is not unusual that when people disappoint us, we begin to dole out love in proportion to their infractions to minimize any future risk. Afraid of going all in . . . we hold back. C. S. Lewis wisely explained the error of this approach in his book *The Four Loves*:

To love at all is to be vulnerable. Love anything and your heart will be wrung and possibly broken. If you want to make sure of keeping it intact you must give it to no one, not even an animal. Wrap it carefully round with hobbies and little luxuries; avoid all entanglements. Lock it up safe in the casket or coffin of your selfishness. But in that casket, safe, dark, motionless, airless, it will change. It will not be broken; it will become unbreakable, impenetrable, irredeemable.*

* C. S. Lewis, *The Four Loves* (New York: Harcourt Brace Jovanovich, 1960), 155.

To love is to be vulnerable. There you have it. We may not like this pairing of love and vulnerability, but I have learned there is simply no way to avoid it. But don't assume that being vulnerable means you are positioned to be violated. Actually, it is more likely that you are positioning yourself to be vindicated, because love never fails. Rest in this, lovely one: You have a Protector who is wild about you.

I love with fearless vulnerability.

The opposite of fear is not faith
or even courage . . . it is love.

FIFTY-TWO

THE WAY OF LOVE

For I am about to do something new.
See, I have already begun! Do you not see it?
I will make a pathway through the wilderness.
I will create rivers in the dry wasteland.

Isaiah 43:19 NLT

Love has the power to make everything that's old new. Everything begins and ends in and with love. Love has the power to create paths in desolate places. Love has the power to water the wild wastelands of our past. Fear does not have these powers. Fear decimates and robs you blind. It will steal your strength, your dreams, your relationships, your finances, your faith, and your hope. Fear wants to taint or take away from you everything that love would freely give. Fear does not appear on the scene occasionally; its attack is as incessant as its timing is flawless.

Fear is a force, the spiritual antithesis of a sound mind and the Holy Spirit's power and love. Fear comes to paralyze you just as surely as God's Spirit comes to release you.

Fear not only robs you of so many opportunities for growth but also wants to steal your perspective of the future. Both love and fear have a plan for your life. One is for good; the other is for harm.

Love, in contrast to fear, is supremely generous. It seeks to restore your relationships, your dreams, and your hope. Every one of us has access to this way of love, promised by God. But it is a mistake to imagine that the new promises of love will stick on the old fabric of fear. God longs to pair the new with *the renewed*. Love seeks to remove fear. Once you have embraced the renewing work of love, you will begin to see everything differently.

> *God's wild love for me removes*
> *my fear and renews my will to love.*

FIFTY-THREE

MULTIFACETED LOVE

> You did not choose me, but I chose you and appointed you that you
> should go and bear fruit and that your fruit should abide.
>
> John 15:16

*D*iamonds symbolize more than just betrothal; they symbolize the attributes of love itself. Like diamonds forged by heat and tectonic forces, love is conceived in wombs of fire and pressure. There can be seasons, years, or even decades when love is buried deep under the surface like a hidden spring. You know it is there. It was planted years ago, deep within the soil of your life, yet you cannot see its beauty or feel its warmth . . . all you sense is its subterranean whisper.

Love in its truest form is not a feeling. It is a choice. This is counterintuitive to a culture that focuses on only the one dimension of love as a *feeling*. But love is multifaceted. Love is why an exhausted mother rouses herself from sleep to respond to the cry of a frightened child. Love is why a father works long hours to provide for his children. And yes, love means there are times when these roles are reversed. The point is that love gives even when it is not returned.

Once Love has chosen, he does not change his mind.

We love because Love chose us. You love because God chose you (1 John 4:19). And our very lives depend on the wondrous truth that the Father loves even when we don't.

I choose to love even when I don't feel loved.

God's love of you is more adamant than a diamond.

FIFTY-FOUR

SEALED

In him you also, when you heard the word of truth, the gospel of your salvation, and believed in him, were sealed with the promised Holy Spirit, who is the guarantee of our inheritance until we acquire possession of it, to the praise of his glory.

Ephesians 1:13–14

We could never make ourselves worthy of God's all-consuming love. I cannot establish myself. You cannot establish yourself. So God has done the work for us.

Now, it is God himself who has anointed us. And he is constantly strengthening both you and us in union with Christ. He knows we are his since he has also stamped his seal of love over our hearts and has given us the Holy Spirit like an engagement ring is given to a bride—a down payment of the blessings to come! (2 Cor. 1:21–22 TPT)

Our modern-day seals, like flimsy wrappers found on vitamin bottles or food products, are different from the seal described in 2 Corinthians. This seal comes from the Greek word *sphragizō* and describes a sevenfold seal:

1. seal of security (we are tightly kept in God's love)
2. seal of authentication (we are marked as God's very own)
3. seal of genuineness
4. seal of ownership
5. seal of approval
6. seal of righteousness
7. seal of promise*

Not one of these seals can be broken by us, because they are tied to Christ's obedience, not our own. Not only are these seals a "hands-off" message to the forces of darkness, but each layer is a divine affirmation of God's betrothal. We cannot reach within ourselves and place these seals upon our hearts. Love reached in and sealed us until the day Love will reveal us.

I am sealed by him and for him.

---

* See footnote on 2 Cor. 1:22 TPT.

FIFTY-FIVE

WHEN HATE ISN'T WRONG

> Love must be sincere. Hate what is evil; cling to what is good.
>
> Romans 12:9 NIV

As a noun, *hate* encompasses such hostile words as *animosity, abhorrence, revulsion,* and *disgust.* When *hate* adopts the form of a verb, it means to loathe, detest, be repulsed by, and despise.

At first glance, it is easy to assume that none of these attributes are in step with a God who not only loves but also is love. Yet, as I searched the Scriptures, I discovered the following. Our Father hates

- everything that undermines justice and truth
- when widows, orphans, and aliens are oppressed
- the abuse of the elderly and the neglect of family
- what perverts his goodness and taints his gifts
- when love twists into selfishness and friends become enemies
- what changes his image and distorts ours

- when evil is called good and the innocent are killed
- when arrogance and pride degrade us

This is not an exhaustive list. The best frame of reference is that God hates all that undermines love, because everything that debases love debases us.

As I searched the Scriptures to understand what God hates, I was shocked to discover more than three thousand words that give context to things that degrade what love seeks to build.

When love is debased, our understanding of God, who is love, is tragically undermined. When God's image is distorted, children who seek a Father are confused. Ultimately, when God hates, it is to protect what he loves. To truly love as God loves, we cannot love what he hates.

God hates what unmakes love.

FIFTY-SIX

LOVE YOUR KING

Do you not know that friendship with the world is enmity with God?
Therefore whoever wishes to be a friend of the world makes himself
an enemy of God.

James 4:4

When the love of God abounds in your life, this earth's pull lessens. As I meditate on God and let him love me, I find that I am easier on myself. When I am easier on myself, I am more loving to others. When I am God-focused and loving, then I am much less likely to pursue empty things, because my relationships fill in the gap.

After reading the verse above, it is hard to imagine anyone choosing to set themselves in opposition to their Creator. James is addressing those who have an eternal covenant but struggle with worldly attachments.

We are to be a friend *to* the world but not friends *with* the world. The first describes how we relate to the world's inhabitants; the second is friendship with its system. You will never have authority over what you are under the sway of. You will never have authority over the things you choose to be entertained by. We are called to acts of compassion for our world. Here's what this means:

We clothe the naked of the world rather than get naked with the world.

We feed the hungry of the world rather than hunger for the world.

We are agents of healing called to be at the bedside of a hurting world rather than in bed with the world.

We are ambassadors of another kingdom, which means we honor our King's commands in this present world. Even when it's uncomfortable and difficult, we choose to love our King over the world.

I choose to be a true friend.

FIFTY-SEVEN

IT STARTS WITH US

If my people who are called by my name humble themselves, and pray and seek my face and turn from their wicked ways, then I will hear from heaven and will forgive their sin and heal their land.

2 Chronicles 7:14

God looks at the posture of his people. This passage outlines an attitude of humility and repentance. Without love, we can be utterly right while being horribly wrong.

Our land needs healing.

This healing begins with us.

Has bemoaning the evils of our day gotten us anywhere? The Bible is clear that a shift happens when we change our posture. It starts when God's people humble themselves, pray, seek God's face, and turn away from their own wicked ways. Do you realize how powerful this is? It doesn't matter who is in power. It doesn't matter what legislation is passed. We don't have to turn everyone else from their evil deeds but simply remove the log from our own eyes and then act accordingly.

Transformation begins as we own our issues and choose to live the truth. Transformation is not measured by the truth we know but is reflected in the truth we live. Love is key in our process of transformation. Without the factors of faith, hope, and love, transformation is impossible. This lack of love is the very reason there has been a move away from holiness and transformation. Each and every day is another chance to follow Jesus and be changed into his likeness.

Because I am fiercely loved,
I'm not afraid to own my issues.

FIFTY-EIGHT

WALK IN MY LIGHT

> But you are the ones chosen by God, chosen for the high calling
> of priestly work, chosen to be a holy people, God's instruments to
> do his work and speak out for him, to tell others of the night-and-
> day difference he made for you—from nothing to something, from
> rejected to accepted.
>
> 1 Peter 2:9–10 Message

None of us are without sin, but that revelation doesn't mean wrong changes to right. Let's revisit the interaction in which Jesus asked the woman caught in adultery if there was anyone left to accuse her:

She said, "No one, Lord." And Jesus said, "Neither do I condemn you; go, and from now on sin no more." (John 8:11)

Jesus did not stop with the mercy of forgiveness ("Neither do I condemn you"); he added in repentance and grace ("Go, and from now on sin no more"). He didn't endorse her lifestyle of adultery. He didn't say, "Don't worry about it, baby girl. All your future sins are forgiven" (even though they were). He didn't say, "I understand you have needs." He said, "Leave your life of shadow and walk in my light."

> Again Jesus spoke to them, saying, "I am the light of the world. Whoever follows me will not walk in darkness, but will have the light of life." (John 8:12)

Rather than leave the darkness for the light, we often change our point of view and call the darkness light. But instead, let's walk in the empathy and holy love that empower others to live lives of freedom. Let's thoughtfully and intentionally invite others to leave behind the darkness of their pasts and follow Jesus into his light.

Through God's grace, I leave the shadows to walk in his light.

FIFTY-NINE

LOVE UNLOCKS IMPRISONED HEARTS

And Jesus, looking at him, loved him, and said to him, "You lack one thing: go, sell all that you have and give to the poor, and you will have treasure in heaven; and come, follow me."

Mark 10:21

When a rich and influential young man asked Jesus what he had to do to inherit eternal life, Jesus responded in love, knowing what was needed to unlock this young man's imprisoned heart. We all have gaps in our lives and blind spots we are unable to see. There are times when love means telling someone what they are missing. When we ask Jesus, he will tell us the truth about ourselves so that our hearts can be true.

Your missing thing might be forgiving someone or trusting that God cares. Whatever it is, the Holy Spirit knows what is needed to unlock your heart. Like us, this rich young ruler was filled with potential, but he held his treasure in the wrong place. Jesus loved him, heard the cry of his heart, and spoke the truth.

Love shows up in our words; it is evident in what we say and what we choose not to say. Love shows up in our tones. We've all said the right thing in the wrong spirit, even the wrong thing in the right spirit, which is still not good.

When we love . . . love finds its voice.

*Because I am fiercely loved,
I receive correction.*

Love speaks so it can be heard.

SIXTY

LOVE BY FAITH

> You have heard that it was said, "You shall love your neighbor and hate your enemy. But I say to you, Love your enemies and pray for those who persecute you."
>
> Matthew 5:43–44

At first glance, the Old Testament approach makes complete sense: Hate your enemy and love your neighbor . . . check. But let's probe a bit deeper. If you are a sibling, a friend, a spouse, a child, or a parent, there will be moments when you have to love by faith. What does this mean? We choose to love even when we don't feel like it. We choose to forgive even when we would rather keep a record of wrongs. Loving enemies takes faith. Praying for people who are attacking you takes faith.

God knew it would be impossible to follow Christ and love the way he loves in our own strength or ability, so he gave each of us a measure of faith. Faith means we can love even when we don't feel love.

When John and I were first married, we would have ridiculous arguments late at night. Exhausted, we would go to bed lying as far away from each other as possible, and we would close our night with, "I forgive you by faith!" At the time, it was our way of saying, "I know I should forgive you, but I'm not ready to let it go, so I'm doing it by faith." It was nothing more than a religious jab, but the principle might have been correct.

When we love by faith and we love in faith, the hurting world sees the Father's heart. When we receive God's trustworthy love for us, then we are well positioned in him to love others.

My love is fueled and strengthened by faith.

SIXTY-ONE

SPEAK TO LOVE

If I speak in the tongues of men and of angels, but have not love, I am a noisy gong or a clanging cymbal. And if I have prophetic powers, and understand all mysteries and all knowledge, and if I have all faith, so as to remove mountains, but have not love, I am nothing.

1 Corinthians 13:1–2

When we speak, we need to ask ourselves some hard questions: Am I speaking out of a place of love, or do I want to be seen and heard?

We all want to be heard. We all have the right to be heard. But when we speak out of hurt, pride, or the pursuit of popularity, being heard becomes its own reward.

Tending our hearts means the motive of love will not be lost in translation. Paul warns us that no matter how profound or divinely inspired our words might seem, without the factor of love, they will fall short like brash and irritating noises.

God alone knows the place from which we speak. In the same way that he sees beyond our appearance into our hearts, he hears more than our words . . . he hears the sound of their source. He hears the melodic or discordant tones in what we say. The three words "I am sorry" are incomparably lovely to him. While the most eloquent of speeches entwined with pride are like fingernails on a blackboard or the screech of banshees, the simplest of sentences woven in love is a symphony.

> *May my words reflect love and humility rather than pride.*

SIXTY-TWO

WORDS OF LIFE

Let no corrupting talk come out of your mouths, but only such as is good for building up, as fits the occasion, that it may give grace to those who hear.

Ephesians 4:29

Words are seeds that can produce life or death. Words are stones that can build or kill. Let's not say we love Scripture and then contradict it with our words. Words are precious—and dangerous.

In the Middle East, stoning was adopted as a form of capital punishment so that no one person could be blamed for the death of the guilty. Stoning happens in our Western world as well. It is just that we practice a different sort of stoning. We don't throw rocks . . . we hurl words. And the more people who take part in the word toss, the less guilty we feel. If everyone is saying something, then no one is guilty, right?

Our culture may affirm this type of reasoning, but we cannot. We answer to a higher purpose and standard. We are not citizens of this world. We are ambassadors of an eternal kingdom. We understand the power of words even if this earth does not. We cannot afford to stone others, because we know better, and those who know better are empowered to do better.

The lamp of God's Word and the leading of his Spirit are essential if we are to navigate this culture that uses words so carelessly. Lies and opinions escalate under the cover of confusion. We need to constantly go to the Source of truth and life to learn how to use words with wisdom.

Let my words build and bring life rather than pain and death.

Set a guard, O LORD, over my mouth;

keep watch over the door of my lips!

—Psalm 141:3

SIXTY-THREE

CONTENTMENT, NOT COMPETITION

> And so it is in the body of Christ. For though we are many, we've all been mingled into one body in Christ. This means that we are all vitally joined to one another, with each contributing to the others. God's marvelous grace imparts to each one of us varying gifts.
>
> Romans 12:5–6 TPT

t is hard to escape the messages and messengers that tell us we are not good enough, young enough, smart enough, fast enough, or rich enough. We are bombarded by others in the hope that we will shrink to their expectations. It is only human nature that we would want to deflect this incessant bullying that implies we are never enough. When this harassment reaches a critical point, some will yield by conforming and copying, while others will rebel as they sling back accusations of their own.

We judge when we feel judged.

We shame when we feel shame.

We hate when we dislike ourselves.

When we've been bankrupted, it is not long before we want to rob others. It is a cycle in which everyone loses and nobody wins. But what if the words of Paul were true?

> But godliness with contentment is great gain. (1 Tim. 6:6)

Godliness is the ability to adopt God's vantage point. This means that just as we acknowledge how he sees others, we embrace how he sees us. Let's turn away from all the detractors and distractions. He has his eyes on us, so we can lift our eyes to him.

In God, I find clarity and perfect contentment.

SIXTY-FOUR

BECKONED TO HIS PRESENCE

> Keep your eyes open, hold tight to your convictions, give it all you've got, be resolute.
>
> 1 Corinthians 16:13 Message

Opinions are so easy to form and so hard to keep to ourselves. If we are not careful, the giving and receiving of opinions can become addictive. We have at our fingertips access to what everyone thinks and feels. At the same time, we have the ability to put any opinion we may hold out into the opinion ocean in seconds. It can be exciting to hear what everyone is saying, especially when they talk to us. But here is where I must warn you: Don't give the opinions of relative strangers too much power over you.

Don't let strangers wound you with the arrows of their careless words. Don't grant your virtual community more access to you than your real one has. You were born to scale mountains, not merely to scan phones. You were born for face-to-face connection, not emojis. Speak God's Word rather than merely echoing it in likes and reposts. None of these things are wrong, but they are far from enough.

Why listen to strangers when you have been invited into an intimate conversation with the Most High? God has beckoned you to come into his presence. It is there, free from comparison and distraction, that the Holy Spirit will breathe life into you and stand you on your feet and fill your mouth with his Word. Make room in your life for God's Spirit.

> *I will not allow the dissenting opinions*
> *of people to drown out*
> *God's words of love for me.*

A generation without convictions is
a generation without transformation.

SIXTY-FIVE

TRAIN MY WORDS

She opens her mouth with wisdom,
and the teaching of kindness is on her tongue.

Proverbs 31:26

*W*ords can be one of the most constructive and one of the most destructive forces on the planet. Yet, just as surely as I have been wounded by the words of people, the Word of God has healed me. This has happened as others have spoken the truth of God's Word into and over my life. It has happened in my times of devotion or prayer when a passage or verse has suddenly arrested me. In a moment's time, everything shifts and my eyes are opened. When we listen to and believe the wisdom of our Creator, we have the chance to learn the right thing the easy way.

Religion that is pure and undefiled before God the Father is this: to visit orphans and widows in their affliction, and to keep oneself unstained from the world. (James 1:27)

We love this verse. But how often do we hear the words of the previous verse quoted?

If anyone thinks he is religious and does not bridle his tongue but deceives his heart, this person's religion is worthless. (James 1:26)

To cultivate a pure and devoted religion, we must learn to ask for God's guidance in training our tongues. We can say, *Lord, may I open my mouth with wisdom and may the teaching of kindness be on my tongue. Help me to use my words to build rather than destroy, to heal rather than wound, to prophesy rather than criticize. Amen.*

> I refuse to allow what I say
> to undermine whose I am.

SIXTY-SIX

DON'T DARE COMPARE

> Not that we dare to classify or compare ourselves with some of those who are commending themselves. But when they measure themselves by one another and compare themselves with one another, they are without understanding.
>
> 2 Corinthians 10:12

Comparison has a pull to it and, if allowed, it will move you away from your truest center. Comparison will attempt to puff you up through the insidious vehicle of pride, or it will push you down through the tyranny of insecurity. Either way, it will not be long before you feel as though you are off-kilter and on the outside looking in.

I hate seeing anyone unintentionally left out. Yet there are times when feeling *on the outside* is the only thing that causes us to *look within*.

Don't you *dare* classify, compare, or commend yourself. Why? It is an action of pride, even if the comparison you make is unfavorable. We all know pride is a precursor to a wipeout.

When we compare ourselves to others or allow comparison to diminish what God wants to do in our lives, pride imbalances one end of the spectrum, while insecurity cripples the other. Both extremes are dangerous. There is but one true measure, the immeasurable Christ, our anointed King of kings.

I refuse to have my wild joy stolen by comparison.

Comparison is the thief of joy.

—Theodore Roosevelt

SIXTY-SEVEN

HEARTS OF INFLUENCE

What good is it for someone to gain the whole world, and yet lose or forfeit their very self?

Luke 9:25 NIV

Recently, I sensed the Holy Spirit asking me, "Lisa, do you want to be popular or influential?"

I answered, "Influential."

To successfully navigate this opinionated world, we need to regularly ask ourselves this question: popular or influential? Maybe you are reading this book because you know you're called to be an influencer for good. This means at times you will take a stand that is less than popular. To gain a bit more understanding, let's define these terms and highlight their differences.

Popular means well liked, prevalent, accepted, fashionable, common, and trendy. There is nothing wrong with being popular, as long as we do not allow popularity to control us. Popularity has its own unique ups and downs, as any of us who went to high school know.

Popularity is built and lost much more quickly than influence. We can incite people, tell them what they want to hear, share what they shouldn't hear, and become popular.

Influential, on the other hand, means powerful, important, persuasive, effective, forceful, and leading. We could be influential and yet relatively unknown in our culture's popular circles. I am convinced that in heaven we will discover that many who are the most influential in the courts of heaven were relatively unknown on the streets of earth. They are those who were willing to sow in secret, who spent more time on their faces talking to God than snapping selfies. To this end, let's set our hearts on being influential.

I seek to please my King rather than to be popular with people.

SIXTY-EIGHT

DON'T SETTLE FOR SAME

Beloved, we are God's children *now*, and what we will be has not yet appeared; but we know that when he appears, we shall be like him, because we shall see him as he is.

1 John 3:2, emphasis added

Even *now* you are his. Being a child of God is not a "one day I will be" promise; it is our present reality. You are alive to grow into all that this adoption will one day mean. There is no need for pretense when you know who you are, and knowing who you are begins with knowing who you belong to. Be a true friend to all of us by being an authentic you. It is time that God's daughters celebrate "unique" and stop settling for "the same" or competing for "more." You actually give others permission to disrespect you when you do not express your true self. People can always discern a counterfeit or copy of the original. Even if they don't see it, they will feel and hear it in the hollowness of your words, actions, and appearance. There is a vast difference between following an example and copying. This is one reason why you get so frustrated when you try to be someone else.

We slight the designation of our Father's love when we deny our unique self-expression. Let's stop wasting our time looking around and allowing constantly changing public opinion to imprint its copycat image or ideas on us. Let's confidently embrace all that God has created us to uniquely reflect.

God is wild about me; therefore,
I can celebrate my uniqueness.

No one can take you out or replace you. You have no rival.

SIXTY-NINE

LOVE AND KNOWLEDGE

I tell you, love your enemies. Help and give without expecting a return. You'll never—I promise—regret it. Live out this God-created identity the way our Father lives toward us, generously and graciously, even when we're at our worst. Our Father is kind; you be kind.

Luke 6:35 Message

Knowing God well should always translate into loving others well. You will never regret a kindness, but the time will come when you will regret any act of cruelty. Living out our identity as a child of God means we begin to follow the patterns of the kingdom rather than the ways of our culture. Not long ago, someone who had maligned me and made my life very difficult for many years reached out to me. She wanted to know if everything between us was all good. She had no way of knowing that over the years many of the things she had said about me had been brought to my attention by others. My first thought was, *Why would you think we would be good after all the bad things you have said?* I was tempted to itemize her infractions just so she would know that I knew. But is that how my Father lives toward me? No. He is love, and love keeps no record of wrongs. I let it go.

As a greater knowledge of who we are in Christ works its way into our lives, we love others the same way that he loves us.

Love is kind, and love never demeans.

Love is gracious, so it never keeps records of wrongs to prove itself right.

Love is generous, which means it gives even when others choose to take.

Love frees the captives by attacking the strongholds that imprison them.

Let's not be those who know about the concept of love without being loving.

God's wild love for me helps me to be untamed in my love for others.

SEVENTY

GLORIOUS MORE

Show no partiality as you hold the faith in our Lord Jesus Christ,
the Lord of glory. . . . If you pay attention to the one who wears the
fine clothing and say, "You sit here in a good place," while you say
to the poor man, "You stand over there," or, "Sit down at my feet,"
have you not then made distinctions among yourselves and become
judges with evil thoughts?

James 2:1, 3–4

The wise do not classify. The wise do not want to be classified. Classifying people is not classy. To classify something is to put it in its place or assign it to a category. Some other terms for this word are to *grade, sort, brand, catalog, rank,* and perhaps the least desirable, *pigeonhole. Merriam-Webster* describes *pigeonhole* as "a neat category that usually fails to reflect actual complexities."*

In life, there are no neat categories. Even the best life is messy. The truth is that everyone's life is much more complex than what we see. And who in

---

* *Merriam-Webster*, s.v. "pigeonhole (*n.*)," accessed October 18, 2021, https://www.merriam
-webster.com/dictionary/pigeonhole.

their right mind would want to be relegated to a box littered with pigeon fallout? Social media is but one of the many opportunities we now enjoy that has the capacity to limit or expand both our prejudices and our perceptions. It is also a medium that threatens to cancel anyone who fails to land within the accepted categories and classes. It is important that we regularly ask ourselves whether we are obeying God's call on our lives or trying to fit in to the currently accepted brand.

Because the fear of man is a snare, the brave do not dare to compare, even if that comparison sees them coming out on top. That position leads to pride, which of course is a precursor to a fall. And just as surely, seeing yourself as less than who God created you to be means you miss the glorious *more* he has for you.

> *Because I am fiercely loved,*
> *I don't dabble in foolish comparisons.*

SEVENTY-ONE

EXCHANGING LIES FOR TRUTH

> For although they knew God, they did not honor him as God or give thanks to him, but they became futile in their thinking, and their foolish hearts were darkened. Claiming to be wise, they became fools.
>
> Romans 1:21–22

The reality of our day weighs on us all. There has never been a generation with more access to information yet with less clarity of purpose. We have some very real challenges when it comes to healthy connections. We develop virtual personas at the expense of our actual relational connections. We have learned to flit from one thing to another, rarely staying long in one place before we are pulled away. The concept of pondering and pausing to worship has become a lost art.

The passage above describes what happens when we refuse to worship God and acknowledge him as our Source.

When we know but do not do, the light within us becomes darkness. Our thought processes go awry or become what the Bible describes as futile, which means wasted and pointless. It is impossible to live well when you cannot think well. Our Western culture has largely encouraged all of us to exchange the glory of the eternal realm for the immediate gratification of what we can buy, touch, and control. We have widely spurned the Creator, who would lift us higher, and turned to worship creation, which draws us lower. But we are ultimately not children of our day—we are children of eternity.

*Because I am fiercely loved,
I honor my Father by being thankful.*

Knowing *about* God is a very different thing than *worshiping* him.

SEVENTY-TWO

KIND BUT NOT SOFT

Or did you think that because he's such a nice God, he'd let you off the hook? Better think this one through from the beginning. God is kind, but he's not soft. In kindness he takes us firmly by the hand and leads us into a radical life-change.

Romans 2:4 Message

For too long, we have tried to distract God from our failings rather than lifting Jesus through our transformed lives. Some sins are easier to hide than others, but this doesn't mean God cannot see what we do. The human tendency is to be hard on sins that are obvious or illegal . . . but what about the more subtle ones, such as slander, envy, strife, gossip, bragging, and greed? Life has taught me the following:

We all need mercy, so it is best to extend mercy.

We all need love, so why not intentionally extend love to others?

We all need hope and to have friendships with those who see the potential of who we might be.

Loving people and extending mercy set all of us up for personal transformation. In the passage above, the apostle Paul explains how life change happens.

God wants to take each and every one of us by the hand and lead us into the life we long for. Our Father's kindness is always an invitation for us to return to truth rather than an endorsement of sin. God ultimately desires to lead us firmly into freedom by the pathway of truth.

> *Because of your fierce love,*
> *I am ready for you to take me*
> *firmly by the hand.*

The hardness of God is kinder than the softness of man, and his compulsion is our liberation.

—C. S. Lewis

SEVENTY-THREE

TRUE NORTH

Who is like you, O Lord, among the gods?
　Who is like you, majestic in holiness,
　awesome in glorious deeds, doing wonders?
You stretched out your right hand;
　the earth swallowed them.

You have led in your *steadfast love* the people whom you
　　have redeemed;
　you have guided them by your strength to your holy
　　abode.

Exodus 15:11–13, emphasis added

Love is our Father's nature. He doesn't love us because he has to; he loves because he cannot *not* love us. God didn't tolerate us in the Old Testament and decide to love us in the New Testament. He didn't decide to love us because Jesus told him to. His love for us was what set our rescue in motion. He gave his Son to express his love for us. His love cannot be conquered by any form of rejection, and it is not undermined by any form of self-loathing. No matter what we do or say, we could never convince him to stop loving us, for, long ago, before we had any say in the matter, he set his love over us as a banner and welcomed us at his table.

> He brought me to the banqueting house,
>   and his banner over me was love. (Song of Sol. 2:4)

I want you to see God's love for you as both a covering and a table spread before you. His love for you is abundant. God doesn't have love *for* us. God *is* love for us. God's love for us is unchanging, invincible, steadfast, and stronger than death. His love is like no other.

God's love is our true north, the one constant by which we can navigate life. His love always leads us home.

God's abundant, fierce love for me is unwavering.

SEVENTY-FOUR

FIERY LOVE

Set me as a seal upon your heart,
    as a seal upon your arm,
for love is strong as death,
    jealousy is fierce as the grave.
Its flashes are flashes of fire,
    the very flame of the Lord.
Many waters cannot quench love,
    neither can floods drown it.
If a man offered for love
    all the wealth of his house,
    he would be utterly despised.

Song of Solomon 8:6–7

These verses expound on the intimate intensity of our Bridegroom's love by declaring the divine unending bonds of passion between lovers.

Does the description of this type of love make you uncomfortable? Maybe it is difficult for you to imagine yourself worthy of someone loving you with this much intensity. Maybe you doubt your capacity to return such love. These words were not penned to make you doubt the love you have experienced or even to cause you to question your capacity to love. This intimate glimpse is given to reveal the passionate type of love you were created for.

It is impossible to measure God's love for us by our human experiences. The lucky in love have known sparks that led to gentle warmth. Others have known sparks that eventually betrayed them when the coals of human love turned to ashes.

Rare is the human love that can be described as a sustained fire. And yet we long for it. If we are honest, we will acknowledge the whisper of our hearts and receive his profound love, as he is our perfect intimate Other.

God's wild love for me is deeper
than I could ever imagine.

SEVENTY-FIVE

FIRST LOVE

We love because he first loved us.

1 John 4:19

God is and will always be our first love. He loved us first, and this first love isn't immature; it is a fierce love. He does not love you with the hope that you will be like someone else. His fierce love has the power to make you fully you. There was never another he compared you to—it was always you. Isn't it wild that even though we first loved others, he first loved us?

Perhaps there are areas of your life in which you have developed a habit of disobedience or inconsistency, and you feel your actions or choices have changed the way God feels about you. That's impossible.

But I do understand. I ran away from his love for far too many years. I didn't understand what his love looked like. There was a time when I thought that if God truly loved me, he would give me what I wanted when I wanted it. When I was young, I imagined that the love of one of his sons would make me happy in my here and now. But God knew better. He knew I had horrible taste in men. I had a tendency to choose men who were hard to please and who turned into those who were hard to keep.

As I look back over my life, I realize God gave me a greater love. He loved me when I said his love wasn't enough. The love of the One who loved me first will always last. My Father looked beyond my fleeting crushes and answered my deepest longing with his love.

Because God loved me first, I know it will last.

The floods of life may threaten, but they cannot drown the love God has for us.

SEVENTY-SIX

LOVED, EVEN WHEN YOU'VE LOST YOUR WAY

He found him in a desert land,
    and in the howling waste of the wilderness;
he encircled him, he cared for him,
    he kept him as the apple of his eye.
Like an eagle that stirs up its nest,
    that flutters over its young,
spreading out its wings, catching them,
    bearing them on its pinions,
the LORD alone guided him.

                        Deuteronomy 32:10–12

Howling wastelands are not good places to be lost in, and they're even worse places to live. When I read these verses, I think about how much I love watching hawks and eagles as they circle the sky and ride the unseen updrafts. They circle to survey their land or to pounce on their prey, but our Creator encircles us to rescue. Life has taught me that God will use our most stirred-up, stressed-out, crazy seasons of life to teach us to fly. We fear that he has dropped us, only later to discover ourselves caught again. Even now, your Creator has the wild thought of yanking you out of any screaming desert wasteland you've lost or hidden yourself in. He has an aerial view of your life and sees the dangers ahead of you as well as the disappointments behind you. He sees the things, people, and places you've hidden from others, and he even sees the things you hide from yourself.

God knows. He is not ignorant of your pain or repulsed by your condition. He is not surprised. He sees you as you wrestle with confusion. You may think he pulls away when he sees you struggle. He doesn't. His Spirit drops down and draws near, waiting, lingering, like a protective lioness watching over her restless cub. And, like a mother eagle, he cheers for you as you escape the confines of the thin shell that you've outgrown. This is the adamantly intimate, steadfast nature of your Creator, who is at once around you and within you.

Intimacy leaves no room for shadowed spaces, so leave behind the desert places. They will always leave you thirsty. Come out of hiding. Your Father sees and loves the *real* you. Trust that this rough season is designed to teach you how to fly.

God is involved in a wild rescue to teach me to fly.

SEVENTY-SEVEN

PREPARING THE SOIL

> We can rejoice, too, when we run into problems and trials, for we
> know that they help us develop endurance. And endurance devel-
> ops strength of character, and character strengthens our confident
> hope of salvation.
>
> Romans 5:3–4 NLT

Trials and tribulations clear the ground and remove what impedes future growth. Even though these encounters can be rough, they are invaluable when it comes to refining and preparing us for future battles and victories.

The discomfort of these experiences serves the purpose of revealing both our strengths and our weaknesses. Collectively and individually, these ordeals work to break up the dry and barren places of our souls in preparation for the new thing or the next season. Without this preparatory groundwork, we run the risk of the water of God's Word running off rather than being absorbed in our lives. Hardened hearts act much like drought-hardened ground that cannot receive water. If the dry soil is not made ready, the rains will run off and you will experience a drought even in the midst of abundance.

Trials also serve to teach us who God is.

There was a time long in the past when popular teachers said that if you were living according to God's Word, then nothing bad could happen to you. I was young and foolish when I first heard this. But this type of teaching only prepares people for life in the shallows. When the waters of life threaten to overwhelm us, this concept will not stand.

Everything you need for life and godliness is waiting to be found in the Word of God, but it is the trials of life that drive us to our knees so that this truth can be worked in and through our lives. In this posture, the Word of God is no longer read as life-enhancing suggestions but as our very words of life.

It is wild, but I find strength and growth in the midst of trials.

SEVENTY-EIGHT

RESURRECTED

> To whom then will you compare me,
>> that I should be like him? says the Holy One.
>
> Lift up your eyes on high and see:
>> who created these?
>
> He who brings out their host by number,
>> calling them all by name;
>
> *by the greatness of his might*
>> *and because he is strong in power,*
>> *not one is missing.*
>
> Isaiah 40:25–26, emphasis added

Nothing lost, nothing wasted, not one piece missing. Buried under so many layers of dust, dirt, and broken stone is yet another page of your story.

Forget for a moment the gravediggers. Push away all thoughts of those who heaped dirt, debris, and rubble in an attempt to bury you alive. Turn from them and ask, *What is it the Enemy wanted buried in my life?*

It may be a hope, a dream, a prayer, or a promise. It may be outside your sight, but don't imagine for a minute that it is off God's mind. Friend, God is in the process of rolling away the stones that have impeded your complete resurrection. He is clearing away the rubble and debris. And all those broken pieces and hard seasons of life that you thought were wasted or lost? The day will come when you will lift your head, look, and discover that he has used each of them to make a beautiful mosaic out of the story of your life. You have been so busy looking down at the mess that you have missed the banner he is weaving over your life.

Lovely one, you are being resurrected.

> *God takes my broken pieces and resurrects them to create something beautiful.*

SEVENTY-NINE

ALL-KNOWING

> I have observed you and what has been done to you in Egypt, and I
> promise that I will bring you up out of the affliction of Egypt.
>
> Exodus 3:16–17

*D*on't imagine that God is unaware just because there is a delayed response to your need. The Israelites sojourned in Egypt for more than four hundred years. A land that had once been a place of refuge and provision had turned on them. A pharaoh rose up who did not remember Joseph or how God had anointed him with the wisdom that was used to preserve the people in a time of famine. This forgetful pharaoh enslaved the Israelites and murdered their male children. It must have felt like even God had forgotten his people. Everything changed when God appeared to Moses. God had heard the cries of an enslaved generation. Because he was aware, he got involved.

As we read the passage above, we immediately see three things: God sees, God knows, and God responds. These three things assure us that God is aware and is taking action on our behalf. Wherever you are at this moment,

I want you to know that you are seen, your heavenly Father knows what is happening, and in the fullness of time he will deliver you from both your affliction and your bondage.

Because he is wildly aware, I can be at peace.

God sees, God knows, God responds.

EIGHTY

THE POWER TO CHOOSE

> Beloved, do not be surprised at the fiery trial when it comes upon you to test you, as though something strange were happening to you. But rejoice insofar as you share Christ's sufferings, that you may also rejoice and be glad when his glory is revealed.
>
> 1 Peter 4:12–13

We have *little* to *no* control over what happens to us or what is said about us, but we are far from helpless when it comes to our actions. You have the power of choice, which gives you total control over how you will choose to respond.

Charles Spurgeon said, "I have learned to kiss the wave that slammed me into the rock." This is an unconventional, unexpected response to the things that catch us unaware.

Spurgeon was not referring to a rocky coastline but to Christ the Rock. Each day is a new opportunity to determine how we will respond to life's waves. If we become defensive, then any issue that comes to light will remain a problem. If we humble ourselves, then the trial allows the Holy Spirit to increase our depth and therefore our capacity for godliness. The challenges of life reveal *what we are made of* without undermining *who we are*. Our identity is established in Christ, based on what he did rather than what we do or have done.

When I watch my granddaughter Sophia play in the waves, I see her revel in the wonder of taking each wave head-on. No matter how many times the waves knock her over and she finds herself submerged . . . it is all a game. Laughing, she finds her feet, wipes her eyes, and emerges, ready to meet the next one. When we see God's hand at work in all that comes our way, we can learn to do the same!

Because I am fiercely loved,
I can dance in the waves that slam me.

EIGHTY-ONE

THE TRUTH UNCHANGING

Enter by the narrow gate. For the gate is wide and the way is easy
that leads to destruction, and those who enter by it are many. For
the gate is narrow and the way is hard that leads to life, and those
who find it are few.

Matthew 7:13–14

*J*esus is the narrow gate that leads to abundant life. Just because the
way is certain, it doesn't mean it won't be hard. It has been argued
that a loving God would include everyone. He did. His invitation
is to all who would *come*. The way was made, but the choice is ours. Which
path will we take? Jesus will not force any of us through the narrow gate. He
will not lie about what it will cost to follow him. He will not say it is easy
when it's not. He knows it is difficult because he has gone before us and is
the very One inviting us to follow, saying, "If you would be my disciples,
deny yourself, take up your cross, and follow" (see Mark 8:34).

You can trust light and truth to be faithful guides. God is light, the Source
of all truth. Light illuminates, and truth remains unchanged. God's truth

does not shift or morph as the balance of human power and thought changes. Truth is more than timeless . . . it is eternal. The road to God begins at the door: Jesus Christ.

Truth does not subject itself to an opinion poll or a popularity contest. The truth might be inconvenient or unpopular, but that does not change the fact that it is truth. Truth is eternal, woven in the Word and statutes of the Most High God.

God is faithful, constant, and true.

EIGHTY-TWO

AS I HAVE LOVED YOU

By this all people will know that you are my disciples, if you have love for one another.

John 13:35

*L*ove well, beautiful friends, and you will live well. Love is our agent of transformation. Our heavenly Father, who is fierce in his love for us, is adamant that we love one another likewise. There are so many people we call enemies who are actually just people who are hurting and desperate to be loved. As followers of Christ, we do not have the option of not loving them. Loving one another is a command rather than a suggestion: "This is my commandment, that you love one another as I have loved you" (John 15:12).

Those five words are the challenge: "as I have loved you."

This means Jesus is our pattern.

I made the mistake of loving others in response to the pattern of how they loved me. The truth is, I wish I would have followed this directive to love better sooner. As God's daughters, we are positioned to love others well because we are so well loved. Looking back over my life, I have no doubt that some of my situations and relationships would have landed differently if I had loved the people involved in the same way Jesus loves me.

While I can't change the past, I am left with clear choices going forward. I can feel bad, and the sadness will stay with me, or I can flip my mistakes into lessons for my future and for others. Once we own our mistakes, they no longer own us. I don't want you to make the same mistakes that I made. Love well and you will not live with regrets.

I am fiercely loved so I can love others as Jesus loves me.

EIGHTY-THREE

AN ORIGINAL LIFE

Since this is the kind of life we have chosen, the life of the Spirit, let us make sure that we do not just hold it as an idea in our heads or a sentiment in our hearts, but work out its implications in every detail of our lives. That means we will not compare ourselves with each other as if one of us were better and another worse. We have far more interesting things to do with our lives. Each of us is an original.

Galatians 5:25–26 Message

We live in an age when everything around us is a tempest of opinions and expectations of others. If you know who you are and whose you are . . . you will stand.

Life in the Spirit is a life led by God. Jesus did only what he saw his Father doing, yet we tend to be content to do what others are doing. A Spirit-led life works its way into every aspect of our lives. It guides how we love, how we forgive, how we believe, and what we hope for. This life begins with the renewing of our minds by reading the Word until the Word begins to speak to us and reorder our lives.

You were not created for comparison. You were created for God's Son. This Spirit-led life is a life of devotion rather than distraction. With each act of obedience in both your intimate and your public life, God will continue to detail your life with his purpose, and his voice will continually grow clearer. Conversely, comparison breeds confusion.

Your life with all of its potential is a God-given entrustment. It would be a shame if all that is in you was like so much treasure and talent buried under the opinions and expectations of strangers. You are not here on earth as a spectator or a duplicator. You have far more important and interesting things to do with your life. It is time you knew this.

I will not be trapped by comparison;
I am an original.

EIGHTY-FOUR

STOP HIDING

Is anything too hard for the LORD?

Genesis 18:14

*I*f God has placed a longing within you, then he will give you the strength to bring it forth. What is the impossible longing that lingers yet in your heart? What is that hope you've nearly given up on?

The above Scripture is a question the angels posed when the impossible promise of a son in their old age was brought to Abraham and Sarah. The mother of our faith, Sarah, was listening in on this conversation and laughed within herself. As for so many of us, the very idea of receiving a promise that had been made decades ago seemed ridiculous and utterly impossible. Too much had happened, too much time had passed, too many mistakes and missteps had been made . . . it was absurd to think of a pregnant old lady. So Sarah was listening in and laughing at a conversation she should have been a part of.

The truth is that there is no substitute for hearing God speak directly to you. You need to jump in on conversations with God that concern your destiny. What has he whispered to you in the past that you now only laugh at? Step outside of the past. We need what you carry in your life. This is not the time for women to hide. Stop hiding, and be part of the conversation.

A lot can happen in a year. It turned out to be a year like no other for Sarah.

Do you realize this year could be the same for you? Maybe your year started in the shadows with you laughing at God's promise, yet, even so, it can end with you daring to hope again. If you are saying any of the following, then you are saying there are some things that are too hard for God:

It's too late.

I'm too young.

I'm too old.

I'm not qualified.

I've made too many mistakes.

I'm fine.

I don't need a dream.

Don't deny your dreams. When you do, the door of your heart shuts. Instead, throw open your heart and embrace all the miraculous wonder you've been invited into.

There is nothing too hard for my wild God.

EIGHTY-FIVE

A SOUL ON FIRE

For this reason I remind you to fan into flame the gift of God, which is in you through the laying on of my hands. For the Spirit God gave us does not make us timid, but gives us power, love and self-discipline.

2 Timothy 1:6–7 NIV

We have been wrapped in the indestructible work of Christ. He is transparent, radiant, magnetic, traced in light, yet as hard as diamond. And the remarkable gift of the Spirit dwells within us even as we dwell in Christ. What exactly does this mean? To answer, allow me to paraphrase Samuel Johnson. Dear one in Christ:

You have a frame of adamant,
And a soul of fire,
No danger should frighten you,
For adversity lifts you higher.*

* Inspired by *The Vanity of Human Wishes* by Samuel Johnson. The text is available at https://www.gutenberg.org/cache/epub/13350/pg13350-images.html.

We have been baptized in the Holy Spirit and with holy fire. Luke 3:16 says, "John answered them all, saying, 'I baptize you with water, but he who is mightier than I is coming, the strap of whose sandals I am not worthy to untie. He will baptize you with the Holy Spirit and fire.'" John's baptism was an outward foreshadowing of what Jesus would work within us. When you were born again, your lifeless heart was quickened by the fiery brilliance of his fierce eternal love. Our God of holy fire consumes the chaff of shadow that would weaken the expression of his love to and through us. His fire encompasses us.

Zechariah 2:5 says, "And I will be to her a wall of fire all around, declares the LORD, and I will be the glory in her midst." I believe this verse speaks of both Jerusalem and Zion the church, and it frames this fire as God's radiant presence within us. Likewise, we are surrounded by God's fiery, protective presence. Because we are surrounded, we can live unafraid.

My wild God is a wall of fire all around me.

EIGHTY-SIX

HIS DIAMONDS

As you come to him, a living stone rejected by men but in the sight of God chosen and precious, you yourselves like living stones are being built up as a spiritual house, to be a holy priesthood.

1 Peter 2:4–5

What you sow does not come to life unless it dies" (1 Cor. 15:36). Hardship serves as your preparation. In so many ways and in so many places, the story of God's daughters has been buried just as, in so many ways, the story of Christ's beautiful bride has been muddied. Even so, remember, daughter of the living God: All that has been hidden will one day be revealed. Just as archaeological finds are continually unearthing the legacy of women within the church, the story of the bride is breaking out again into the light.

We are those women.

We are his bride.

His diamonds.

His priceless treasure.

He is our Adamant, our Cornerstone, our Truth.

He is the Rock that follows us through each of our wildernesses.

Lift your life and honor the Stone from which you were hewn. Live in wonder of the immovable, invincible, impervious, the Cornerstone who longs to astound you with his loving faithfulness. You are imprinted on his heart, and his words are spoken in kindness.

Be true to him in this universe of opinions and controversies, for you are marked for the eternal realm. Honor him, brave one, with the strength of your heart and the length of your days. Tell others of his fierce love. Honor his hand in your life with the royal authority of his Word and the anointing of his Holy Spirit.

I am wild treasure faceted by God's fierce love.

181

EIGHTY-SEVEN

SEIZE YOUR MOMENT

You saw me before I was born.
    Every day of my life was recorded in your book.
Every moment was laid out
    before a single day had passed.

Psalm 139:16 NLT

You have been seeded with a stunning story of promise. Your heavenly Father wrote out the intimate details of your life in his book long before you drew your first breath.

He wrote your life with living letters. No one else can live your story. It is time your pages came alive. Living the story lines written for others will leave what the Spirit has written for you unfulfilled. Each and every one of us has a specific course and destiny. The Holy Spirit's direction is essential if you are going to live the life you've been given to its fullest.

Your future is now.

You have today, this one point in time. None of us is promised tomorrow, but you know this moment is yours. And the power of your choices can redeem all your moments.

The book of your life can remain closed, or you can continue to turn the pages. Listen to Paul's message to the Galatians:

Make a careful exploration of who you are and the work you have been given, and then sink yourself into that. Don't be impressed with yourself. Don't compare yourself with others. Each of you must take responsibility for doing the creative best you can with your own life. (Gal. 6:4–5 Message)

You are God's daughter. You are his ambassador. The work we have each been given is called the ministry of reconciliation.

I embrace the beautifully wild story
God is writing with my life.

EIGHTY-EIGHT

WELL DONE

Well done, my good and faithful servant. You have been faithful
in handling this small amount, so now I will give you many more
responsibilities. Let's celebrate together!

Matthew 25:21 NLT

When this earthly life is finished, we all hope to hear *well done*. The word *well* describes *how* we do whatever it is we are called to do. There is no such thing as *perfectly done* in the scheme of human life or love. There are only imperfect people doing it well. The word *well* is a gift to each of us. It is a word that means healthy and sound. It describes people who fail and fall but who get back up each time. This life simply requires that we get back up one more time than we fall. This is the posture we need to adopt if we want to develop a depth that will sustain us.

> For the lovers of God may suffer adversity
>> and stumble seven times,
>>> but they will continue to rise over and over again.
>>>> (Prov. 24:16 TPT)

People tend to measure others by how many times they fall, but our Father is watching for how many times we will get back up. Adversity is life's university. The cost of each class's tuition can be measured by what it takes for you to get up *just one more time*. But with each commitment to rise, we learn what it means to live this life and this faith *well*.

I am dedicated to living my one life well.

Brave daughter, don't miss the fact that the extraordinary hides within how we handle the ordinary.

EIGHTY-NINE

FAITHFUL TO THE END

> I have fought an excellent fight. I have finished my full course *with all my might* and I've kept my heart full of faith.
>
> 2 Timothy 4:7 TPT

The *done* part of *well done* is all about the *completion*. The Bible is rife with stories and parables about finishing well—or poorly. There is Noah, a man whose great boat-building project took years (Gen. 6). There is Samson, who, despite a colossal blunder, finished in a spectacular show of divine strength (Judg. 15). There are Peter and Paul. Peter's denial of Christ and Paul's persecution of Christ paved the way for the power of their ministries (Matt. 26; Acts 7–8). In contrast, there is the man who started his building without first counting the costs. He began well but then was mocked for not finishing well (Luke 14:27–29). Then there is the servant who was entrusted with one talent, which he decided to bury until his master's return. Coins do not grow in the ground, so when he dug it up, all he had was what he'd started with. Ending where he began earned him the label of "wicked" and a place on the outside looking in (Matt. 25:14–30).

What all these stories tell us is that persistent, faithful, steady obedience will always win out over casual and inconsistent bursts of activity and enthusiasm. Even when we stumble along the way, if we pick ourselves up and head in the right direction, God will bring us home.

Journeying well in this life requires us to dig deep and *finish* what we start, faithfully.

Because I am fiercely loved,
I will be fiercely faithful to the very end.

It is ultimately not about our *pace* but about *how we finish* our race.

NINETY

A PRAYER FOR
THE FIERCELY LOVED

hen I first believed in Christ, John gave me the following Scriptures as a promise, and it wasn't long before the words of this passage became a prayer. Just as these words of the apostle Paul were gifted to me, I want to gift his words to you. The church in Ephesus was young and birthed in a world that was completely at odds with the Judaic culture. The new believers there found their new way of life completely at odds with the ideology of their day. In so many ways, I feel you and I have found ourselves alive in a day and age of reasoning that can feel the same way. I want to close out our time together by weaving Ephesians 1:15–23 into a prayer.

Dearest fiercely loved one,

Because I have heard of your faith in the Lord Jesus and your love toward all the saints (not just the ones you've met but those you will never meet and those you choose to love even when they are less than

*kind). For all these reasons and more, I am thanking our heavenly
Father for you and remembering you in my prayers. I am believing that
the God of our Lord Jesus Christ, the Father of glory, may give you the
Spirit of wisdom and of revelation in the knowledge of him, that the
more you know his fierce love, pure holiness, and righteous judgments,
the more discerning you would become. This way, the eyes of your heart
are enlightened, that you may personally know what is the hope to which
he has called you, what are the riches of his glorious inheritance in the
saints, and what is the immeasurable greatness of his power toward us
who believe, according to the working of his great might that he worked
in Christ when he raised him from the dead and seated him at his right
hand in the heavenly places, far above all rule and authority and power
and dominion, and above every name that is named, not only in this age
but also in the one to come. And he put all things under his feet and gave
him as head over all things to the church, which is his body, the fullness
of him who fills all in all.*

You are his fiercely loved daughter who courageously hopes in him. Your
life is under his authority. He is not unaware or unconcerned. Not only does
he love you; he cares about the great and the small, the unseen and the seen.
He is wild for you. Rest in this, dear one.

> *Because I am fiercely loved,
> all my hope is in him.*

LISA BEVERE has spent more than three decades empowering women of all ages to find their identity and purpose. She is a *New York Times* bestselling author and an internationally known speaker. Her previous books, which include *Fight Like a Girl*, *Lioness Arising*, *Girls with Swords*, *Without Rival*, and *Godmothers*, are in the hands of millions worldwide. Lisa and her husband, John, are the founders of Messenger International, an organization committed to developing uncompromising followers of Christ who transform their world. Learn more at LisaBevere.com and MessengerX.com.